Vol. XIV No. 3

Adult Bible Class
Large-Print Edition

SUMMER QUARTER June, July, August 2023

Editorial 2

Christ Proclaims the Kingdom

UNIT I: Understanding God's Kingdom

June 4—Upside-Down Kingdom—Matt. 5:1-16	4
June 11—A Perfect Kingdom—Matt. 5:17-18, 21-22, 27-28, 38-39, 43-44	9
June 18—A Victorious Kingdom—Mark 3:13-19; 6:6*b*-13	14
June 25—Growing God's Kingdom—Matt. 13:24-33	19

UNIT II: Responding to God's Kingdom

July 2—Praying to God—Luke 11:1-13	24
July 9—Accept God's Invitation!—Luke 14:7-11, 15-24	29
July 16—A Warning for the Hard-Hearted—Luke 16:19-31	34
July 23—Separating the Sheep and the Goats—Matt. 25:31-46	39
July 30—Ears to Hear—Matt. 13:9-17	43
Aug. 6—Forgiving One Another—Matt. 18:21-35	47

UNIT III: Entering God's Kingdom

Aug. 13—A Story of Forgiveness—Luke 15:11-24	51
Aug. 20—God's Gracious Rewards—Matt. 20:1-16	55
Aug. 27—God's Great Mercy—Luke 18:9-14	59
Paragraphs on Places and People	63
Daily Bible Reading	64

Editor in Chief: Kenneth Sponsler

Edited and published quarterly by
THE INCORPORATED TRUSTEES OF THE GOSPEL WORKER SOCIETY
UNION GOSPEL PRESS DIVISION
Rev. W. B. Musselman, Founder

Price: $5.79 per quarter*
*shipping and handling extra
ISBN 978-1-64495-296-2

This material is part of the "Christian Life Series," copyright © 2023 by Union Gospel Press. All rights reserved. No portion of this publication may be reproduced in any form or by any means without written permission from Union Gospel Press, except as permitted by United States copyright law. Edited and published quarterly by The Incorporated Trustees of the Gospel Worker Society, Union Gospel Press Division. Mailing address: P.O. Box 301055, Cleveland, Ohio 44130-0915. Phone: 216-749-2100. www.uniongospelpress.com

EDITORIAL

The Majesty of Christ's Church

BY JOHN LODY

Jesus proclaimed, "Upon this rock I will build my church; and the gates of hell shall not prevail against it" (Matt. 16:18). The "rock" is Peter's inspired confession that Jesus is in fact "the Christ, the Son of the living God" (vs. 16). Verse 18 is the first of over a hundred occurrences of the word "church" in the New Testament. Christ's church is the present, visible manifestation of Christ's kingdom in the hearts of His true disciples. Indeed, Christ will most certainly one day return and establish His kingdom on earth (cf. Acts 1:9-11; Rev. 11:15). But from now until then, the church on earth is the dominant expression of His kingdom (cf. Luke 17:20-21; I Cor. 6:19-20; I Pet. 2:5). As such, it is the main event in God's redemptive plan. It is not God's "plan B" after some other plan had failed. On the contrary, it has always been God's explicit intent to summon the full number of His elect from both the Jews and the Gentiles through Christ (cf. Eph. 1:4).

The first principle of Christ's church that we need to realize is that it is a spiritual kingdom. This should never be construed to mean that it is somehow less real than any future earthly kingdom. Nor should we ever assume that its being spiritual makes it somehow less important. In actuality, the exact opposite is true. As Paul wrote, "We look not at the things which are seen, but at the things which are not seen: for the things which are seen are temporal; but the things which are not seen are eternal" (II Cor. 4:18; cf. Heb. 11:3). The entire material realm was created from nothing and is even now sustained by God alone, who is a sovereign, invisible Spirit (cf. John 4:24; Col. 1:15-17; I Tim. 1:17). Without God's constant sustaining spiritual power, the material world would cease to exist!

The church derives its spiritual power from the Holy Spirit, the Third Person of the Trinity. He is the saving power behind the gospel as it is preached. It is He who draws the hearts of sinners to saving faith and repentance. It is He who indwells the church, the body and bride of Christ. Moreover, He Himself indwells each individual believer. He makes both the church and each individual Christian the temple of God. It is the Holy Spirit's power that guides, directs, and sanctifies both the church and each Christian's life.

It is the saving, sanctifying power of the Holy Spirit that drives the progress of God's kingdom in the church to its assured future triumph. The Holy Spirit calls the servants of Christ to build up God's kingdom to its fullness. He ordains pastors, teachers, elders, deacons, and servants in every place that the church needs to make and build up disciples from spiritual babyhood to the fullness of Christ's image in them. He also sends missionaries to carry the gospel to the ends of the earth so that one day, the kingdoms of this world will "become the kingdoms of our Lord, and of his Christ; and he shall reign for ever and ever" (Rev. 11:15).

The majesty of the church is that it does not extend its influence through violence or military force. The church wars not against flesh and blood, that is, against human beings, but against the spiritual powers of sin, wickedness, and injustice that have corrupted God's good and holy creation. People are never the primary enemies of the church or its gospel; rather, they are hostages, prisoners who have been deceived into serving the real enemy. The principal enemy is Satan and his minions, who constantly prowl about seeking whom they may devour (cf. I Pet. 5:8).

The church's commission is not to destroy, but to capture the hearts of Satan's hostages through God's grace and love for lost sinners. It accomplishes this by being the instruments of God as He transforms them into God's friends and adopts them as His children, bringing new life to those who were dead in their sins and making them truly alive again by the power of His Holy Spirit. Through faith, Christ's church overcomes the world (cf. John 16:33; I John 5:4-5)!

In closing, I would challenge you to read and meditate upon the words of the great old hymn, "The Church's One Foundation," by Samuel J. Stone. It presents an accurate and heart-moving picture of Christ's church as His bride and kingdom. Let us take a closer look at this hymn and see how it squares beautifully with what we have seen of the teachings of Scripture.

The opening line of the hymn declares, "The church's one Foundation is Jesus Christ her Lord." The first verse goes on to celebrate the fact that the church was purchased through the sacrifice of Christ.

Because of what Christ has done for His people, they enjoy a wonderful unity. Stone's hymn memorably sets forth that unity, referring to the church's "charter of salvation, one Lord, one faith, one birth. He further declares that "one holy Name she blesses, partakes one holy food. And to one hope she presses, with every grace endued."

The unity the church enjoys among her members is due to her unity with the Triune God. The spiritual relationship of God's people extends not only all over the world but through all of time as well. This is the sense in which the hymn refers to the "mystic sweet communion" that believers even now enjoy with those saints who have already died--not, of course, in any occult or visible way, but rather in the sure hope that we will one day enjoy fellowship in the eternal kingdom of God with all true believers.

"The Church's One Foundation" was written in the midst of theological controversy concerning the reliability of the Scriptures and the fundamental truths it contains. Such controversies continue today. Samuel Stone wrote with the confidence that God's church and kingdom would remain intact. We share in that confidence because Jesus Christ remains the Rock upon which they are built.

LESSON 1 — JUNE 4, 2023

Scripture Lesson Text

MATT. 5:1 And seeing the multitudes, he went up into a mountain: and when he was set, his disciples came unto him:

2 And he opened his mouth, and taught them, saying,

3 Blessed *are* the poor in spirit: for theirs is the kingdom of heaven.

4 Blessed *are* they that mourn: for they shall be comforted.

5 Blessed *are* the meek: for they shall inherit the earth.

6 Blessed *are* they which do hunger and thirst after righteousness: for they shall be filled.

7 Blessed *are* the merciful: for they shall obtain mercy.

8 Blessed *are* the pure in heart: for they shall see God.

9 Blessed *are* the peacemakers: for they shall be called the children of God.

10 Blessed *are* they which are persecuted for righteousness' sake: for theirs is the kingdom of heaven.

11 Blessed are ye, when *men* shall revile you, and persecute *you,* and shall say all manner of evil against you falsely, for my sake.

12 Rejoice, and be exceeding glad: for great *is* your reward in heaven: for so persecuted they the prophets which were before you.

13 Ye are the salt of the earth: but if the salt have lost his savour, wherewith shall it be salted? it is thenceforth good for nothing, but to be cast out, and to be trodden under foot of men.

14 Ye are the light of the world. A city that is set on an hill cannot be hid.

15 Neither do men light a candle, and put it under a bushel, but on a candlestick; and it giveth light unto all that are in the house.

16 Let your light so shine before men, that they may see your good works, and glorify your Father which is in heaven.

NOTES

Upside-Down Kingdom

Lesson Text: Matthew 5:1-16

Related Scriptures: Psalm 24:1-6; Isaiah 66:1-2;
Luke 6:20-26; Hebrews 11:36-38

TIME: A.D. 28   PLACE: mountain near Capernaum

GOLDEN TEXT—"Blessed are they which do hunger and thirst after righteousness: for they shall be filled" (Matthew 5:6).

Lesson Exposition

THE INDIVIDUAL HEART—
Matt. 5:1-6

Spiritual instruction (Matt. 5:1-2). The implication in these verses is that Jesus drew away from the multitudes in order to instruct His disciples privately. When we read Matthew 7:28, though, we conclude that many had gathered and listened in while He taught, so that by the end of His teaching session there was another multitude present.

There seem to have been three levels of followers throughout Jesus' ministry. There were the twelve men He chose to prepare for taking the gospel throughout the world; there was a larger group of believers also sometimes referred to as disciples; and, finally, there were the crowds that followed Him out of curiosity or with some other motive. From among the Twelve, there were three we sometimes refer to as His inner circle of disciples. These were Peter, James, and John. They shared some experiences that none of the others did.

Spiritual need (Matt. 5:3-4). The Beatitudes form the introduction to Jesus' message, and there is a parallel development of their thoughts in the body of the message. They are also progressive in thought, with each one logically following the one preceding it. They are not meant to be cute sayings but rather truths to be lived. The word "blessed" literally means "happy," but it is more than a surface emotion. It is a deep sense of being blessed by God in a way that leads to genuine contentment and peace in the heart.

The first characteristic of righteousness mentioned is being poor in spirit. This does not refer to those who are physically poor. It speaks of the person who recognizes that in himself there is no merit or righteousness, that is, nothing to make him worthy of heaven. It is the recognition that one is unable to become righteous without help from God.

Those who mourn (vs. 4) are those who see their spiritual poverty and become deeply sorrowful over it. This is a godly sorrow that leads to genuine repentance.

Spiritual maturity (Matt. 5:5-6). It is wrong to equate meekness with weakness. Meekness is sometimes defined as strength under control. A meek person can in reality be a very powerful person, but he is one who is spiritually mature and gracious enough to use his strength positively and constructively instead of negatively and destructively. Meekness is not looking down on oneself and feeling unworthy, either. A meek person realizes that God has given him certain authority as His child and that he is free to use it.

Such a person does, however, submit completely to the will of God and uses his freedom and authority only as God wants. It is this unquestioning submission that most characterizes the meek person. Both Moses and Paul were meek (cf. Num. 12:3; II Cor. 10:1), and in both of them we see strong leadership abilities used under the guiding hand of God. Neither sought personal gain. Both wanted people to know the joy of obeying God. The reward for such submission will be realized in the coming kingdom, when Christ rules on earth.

It is characteristic of the meek that they have an appetite for the things that make them more pleasing to God and more conformed to His righteousness. We know what it is to be very hungry or thirsty. When we experience either, our body craves what it has been missing and desperately needs. Food or drink becomes the center of our thoughts and the focus of our determination. We reach a point at which nothing else matters as much as satisfying the hunger or thirst driving us to distraction.

This kind of insatiable longing for righteousness will be answered. We will find ourselves being completely satisfied as we read God's Word, pray, worship, sing, and study what others have written about His Word.

RELATIONSHIPS WITH OTHERS—Matt. 5:7-12

Spiritual outreach (Matt. 5:7-8). God is merciful, and we should be most grateful that He is! On our own we deserve nothing, and apart from His grace and mercy we would never have the hope of heaven. The person who exhibits mercy will be rewarded with mercy.

An often heard statement is that God's mercy is His withholding from us what we deserve. We deserve hell because of our sin, but God removes that punishment from us when we receive His Son as Saviour. Our natural tendency is to be selfish and unforgiving toward those who have wronged us. We want them to get what they deserve because of what they have done. The righteous attitude is a forgiving attitude, and as we exercise it, we will have a greater sense of God's forgiveness.

Those of us who have experienced God's mercy have been cleansed from our sins. We need to live in purity of heart, which reflects the status we have with God. Perhaps the climactic truth in the Beatitudes is that the pure in heart will see God someday.

Spiritual privileges (Matt. 5:9-10). We live in a troubled world in which people long for peace. We know there will not be real peace among nations until the Lord Jesus reigns on earth. But we also know that individuals who have trusted in Jesus Christ as their personal Saviour are at peace with God regarding their eternal destiny and that it is possible for them to live at peace with others. Furthermore, it is the person who loves the Lord and is endeavoring to live according to His Word who can help others find peace.

Jesus then spoke about suffering from oppression because of our beliefs. The ability to endure persecution gracefully is evidence of a genuine faith.

Spiritual endurance (Matt. 5:11-12). The proper perspective on persecution is amplified in these verses. It is a blessing to know our testimony is so effective that it is noticed and opposed by those who do not believe. The followers to whom Jesus originally spoke these words were going to experience tremendous opposition from the Roman government. By the time of the apostle Paul's ministry, Nero was the emperor, and he displayed a deep-seated hatred of Christians. While we know Nero as a notorious emperor, others would be just as bad.

RELATIONSHIPS WITH THE WORLD—Matt. 5:13-16

Spiritual influence (Matt. 5:13-14). Three figures are used to illustrate the believer's influence on the world: salt, light, and a city on a hill. Salt does several things. It adds flavor, it causes thirst, it acts as a preservative, it melts ice, and it helps in the healing of wounds if used properly. As believers, we have an opportunity to make a difference in the lives of people.

We should improve life by providing a spiritual flavor unknown by the unsaved. We should cause others to thirst for the joy of life we possess. We should be a means of preserving and maintaining godliness in the midst of a dark, godless society. We should provide the warmth that melts hard, resistant hearts.

Pure salt will maintain its flavor. In Israel, however, most of the salt was mixed with other minerals. In certain circumstances this mixture could lose its flavor, making it worthless for seasoning. When that happened, it was used to cover roads to keep the grass from growing there. It is possible for us to become useless to others if our hearts are cold and uncaring.

Spiritual light (Matt. 5:15-16). Jesus chose to expand on the illustration of light by explaining how light is most effectively used. You should notice that Jesus did not say this is what believers should be but what they already are. Because we are in Christ, we are very different from the world. Every true believer is a light in this dark world simply because he knows the truth.

Since believers are lights in this world, any believer who does not function as a light in revealing spiritual reality and truth is actually acting contrary to his new nature. Such a person is like the light that has been lit and then hidden under a basket, offering no help to anyone in the home. Such a light is useless to everyone present, and a Christian with no testimony is useless to his Saviour and those near him who are separated from God. We are challenged, therefore, to let our testimonies shine for God.

Our faith is most easily seen through our good works. When unsaved people can clearly see that we live with a higher and more noble standard than do those of the world, they will be drawn to what we have.

—Keith E. Eggert.

QUESTIONS

1. Who was listening to Jesus at the beginning of the Sermon on the Mount, and how did that change?
2. What three basic types of followers do we see in Jesus' ministry?
3. What is the true meaning of "blessed" in these verses?
4. What does "poor in spirit" (Matt. 5:3) refer to, and how does mourning tie in with it?
5. What is the meek person like?
6. What does it mean to "hunger and thirst after righteousness" (vs. 6)?
7. What is it about us that keeps us from being naturally merciful, and why should showing mercy be important to us?
8. What are the characteristics of a peacemaker?
9. What three pictures illustrate the effect we should have on the world?
10. Why did Jesus not say we *should* be lights in this world?

—Keith E. Eggert.

PRACTICAL POINTS

1. We must always see ourselves as weak and totally dependent on the Lord (Matt. 5:1-4).
2. To be like Christ means we must be gentle in all our relationships (vs. 5).
3. A desire to live righteously will be seen in our merciful treatment of others (vss. 6-7).
4. We who know the peace of God must seek to share it with others (vss. 8-9).
5. We should see persecution for our faith as an opportunity to honor the Lord (vss. 10-12).
6. Good works are not a means of elevating ourselves, but a way of glorifying God (vss. 13-16).

—*Jarl K. Waggoner.*

RESEARCH AND DISCUSSION

1. Is "blessedness," or true happiness, something we should pursue, or is it the result of pursuing other things (Matt. 5:1-11)?
2. Why is meekness not often considered a virtue today? In what ways can we actively practice it?
3. How can we pursue righteousness without becoming legalistic or self-righteous?
4. In what practical ways can we be "peacemakers" in our world?
5. Should we expect to be persecuted for our faith (Matt. 5:12; cf. John 5:18; I Pet. 4:12-13)? Should we be concerned if we experience no persecution?
6. Can you cite outstanding examples of people who let their light "shine before men" (Matt. 5:16)?

—*Jarl K. Waggoner.*

Golden Text Illuminated

"Blessed are they which do hunger and thirst after righteousness: for they shall be filled" (Matthew 5:6).

The term "blessed" refers to happiness, and Jesus singled out certain people who would be given that wonderful blessing because of something in their lives. The ones specifically referred to in our golden text are those who recognize sin for what it is and for what it does to the human soul. They are those whose lives were once filled with sin.

Those who see sin for what it is and hate what it does to the human condition are those who long for something better. They know there is something better, but they also recognize their inability to change. They long to be righteous but find that righteousness eludes them.

Jesus can pronounce a blessing on someone who thirsts and hungers after righteousness because such a person is drawn to Christ. Anyone who comes to Him is welcomed with open arms (John 6:37). He finds in Christ freedom from the eternal penalty of sin, acceptance and worth as a person, a guiding light in a world dark with sin, a power to live so that God can bless, a way to escape the temptations that continue to dog the path of a believer, and a Friend who knows what it is like to be human.

To such a person comes an inner sense of joy and happiness that may be dampened on occasion but, like an eternal flame, is never extinguished. It is called eternal life. Is your own life lit by such a flame?

—*Darrell W. McKay.*

LESSON 2 JUNE 11, 2023

Scripture Lesson Text

MATT. 5:17 Think not that I am come to destroy the law, or the prophets: I am not come to destroy, but to fulfil.

18 For verily I say unto you, Till heaven and earth pass, one jot or one tittle shall in no wise pass from the law, till all be fulfilled.

21 Ye have heard that it was said by them of old time, Thou shalt not kill; and whosoever shall kill shall be in danger of the judgment:

22 But I say unto you, That whosoever is angry with his brother without a cause shall be in danger of the judgment: and whosoever shall say to his brother, Raca, shall be in danger of the council: but whosoever shall say, Thou fool, shall be in danger of hell fire.

27 Ye have heard that it was said by them of old time, Thou shalt not commit adultery:

28 But I say unto you, That whosoever looketh on a woman to lust after her hath committed adultery with her already in his heart.

38 Ye have heard that it hath been said, An eye for an eye, and a tooth for a tooth:

39 But I say unto you, That ye resist not evil: but whosoever shall smite thee on thy right cheek, turn to him the other also.

43 Ye have heard that it hath been said, Thou shalt love thy neighbour, and hate thine enemy.

44 But I say unto you, Love your enemies, bless them that curse you, do good to them that hate you, and pray for them which despitefully use you, and persecute you.

NOTES

A Perfect Kingdom

Lesson Text: Matthew 5:17-18, 21-22, 27-28, 38-39, 43-44

Related Scriptures: Acts 14:8-18; Romans 9:30—10:4;
I Corinthians 3:11-15; James 2:10-13

TIME: A.D. 28   PLACE: mountain near Capernaum

GOLDEN TEXT—"Think not that I am come to destroy the law, or the prophets: I am not come to destroy, but to fulfil" (Matthew 5:17).

Lesson Exposition

Some have suggested that Matthew presents Jesus as the new Moses. Just as there are five books of Moses (the law), so there are five major discourses in Matthew. Just as Moses received God's law on a mountain, so Christ delivered His new law from a mountain. Matthew 5 through 7 is called the Sermon on the Mount, a small portion of which we study this week.

It is also noteworthy that there are numerous contrasts in this sermon between what the rabbis said the law taught and what Christ declared to be true. The Master Teacher was interpreting the Mosaic law in light of truths that He revealed as the Son of God.

THE LAW FULFILLED—
Matt. 5:17-18

Not to destroy (Matt. 5:17). In the verses that follow this part of the Sermon on the Mount, Christ made several contrasts between His teaching and the interpretation of the scribes and Pharisees. He addressed such topics as murder (vss. 21-22), adultery (vss. 27-30), divorce (vss. 31-32), and the taking of oaths (vss. 33-37).

While some may have thought that Christ came to destroy the Law and the Prophets, this was not the case at all; rather, He came to fulfill them. "By fulfillment is meant not just the carrying out of predictions but the accomplishment of the intention of the Law and the Prophets. In contrast to the Pharisees, Jesus brought out the true and deeper meaning of the Law, and he actually lived up to its intention" (Allen, ed., *Broadman Bible Commentary*, Broadman).

All will be fulfilled (Matt. 5:18). Christ declared that the minutest details of the law would be fulfilled in Him. A "jot," or yod, was the smallest letter in the Hebrew alphabet. The smallest Greek letter, iota, is still used today to express something very small. The "tittle" was the least stroke of a pen that could change one letter to another. The thrust of Christ's statement was that every part of the Law and the Prophets would be fulfilled in Him before the end of time.

THE LAW INTERPRETED—
Matt. 5:21-22, 27-28

Do not kill (Matt. 5:21). From the beginning of time, man has understood that there was a prohibition against the taking of human life (Gen.

4:10; 9:6). This was reinforced by the teaching of the Ten Commandments (Ex. 20:13) and the body of the Mosaic Law, which required capital punishment for this and certain other crimes (21:12-17; 22:18-20).

The warning about being in "danger of the judgment" (Matt. 5:21) had to do with the system of courts and judges found in ancient Israel (Deut. 16:18; 19:11-20). As in modern times, those who took the lives of others were subject to the criminal justice system under which they lived.

Do not be angry (Matt. 5:22). Though the human propensity to get angry is not wrong in itself, many do so "without a cause." Again, the mention of "judgment" likely refers to the local judges, not necessarily the final judgment. The point of our Lord, however, was to show that both overt acts (such as murder) and the inner motivation that leads to such acts (anger) are serious matters.

The meaning of the Aramaic word "Raca" is somewhat uncertain, but it could be translated "empty-head" or "good-for-nothing." It was a term of contempt reserved for those considered utterly worthless.

The Greek word for "council" is the word used for the Great Sanhedrin, the highest court in the land.

Again, Christ's point was that treating others with contempt puts one in grave danger. And to declare another a fool was to place one's soul in danger of eternal punishment (Matt. 5:22).

"The word, *Gehenna,* rendered *hell* . . . is the Greek representative of the Hebrew Ge-Hinnom, or Valley of Hinnom, a deep, narrow glen to the south of Jerusalem, where, after the introduction of the worship of the fire-gods by Ahaz, the idolatrous Jews sacrificed their children to Molech. Josiah formally desecrated it [and] it became the common refuse place of the city, into which the bodies of criminals, carcasses of animals, and all sorts of filth were cast. From its depth and narrowness, and its fire and ascending smoke, it became the symbol of the place of the future punishment of the wicked" (Vincent, *Word Studies,* Eerdmans).

Lust forbidden (Matt. 5:27-28). "Thou shalt not commit adultery" (Ex. 20:14). What is at the root of this prohibition? Is it not keeping one's mind and heart pure? While a man may keep himself from actually physically committing adultery, it is much more difficult to keep one's thought life pure. Christ went to the very heart of the matter, the lustful mind.

"Jesus is not saying that lustful desires are identical to lustful deeds, and therefore a person might just as well go ahead and commit adultery. The desire and the deed are not identical, but, spiritually speaking, they are equivalent. The 'look' that Jesus mentioned was not a casual glance, but a constant stare with the purpose of lusting" (Wiersbe, *Bible Exposition Commentary*, Victor).

THE LAW OF LOVE—
Matt. 5:38-39, 43-44

Eye for eye (Matt. 5:38). The concept of an eye for an eye comes from the Mosaic Law (Ex. 21:23-25; Lev. 24:20). This law did not justify personal vengeance or vindictiveness, however. In fact, the purpose of this law was not just to secure justice in the case of an offense; it also was designed to restrict personal and unlimited retaliation against an offender (Deut. 19:4-7).

Turn the other cheek (Matt. 5:39). The Lord's statement "Resist not evil" might give us the impression that we are to allow evil to go unchecked in our world. This command applies to individuals, however, not government. In short, it means the Christian must not respond to evil with evil. When tempted to retaliate, we must rise above a vengeful spirit. The only way evil can be conquered is to overcome it with good (Rom. 12:16-21).

When treated badly, most find it difficult to turn the other cheek. Doing so takes great strength and courage. When hurt, we think that it will make us feel better to get back at the one who caused us pain, but it does not.

Love your neighbor (Matt. 5:43-44). While the law did say, "Thou shalt love thy neighbour" (Lev. 19:18), it did not state that one's enemies were to be hated. Even so, this was a common teaching among the Jewish rabbis, who drew a sharp distinction between one's neighbor and one's enemy. "It is astonishing, that the scribes fell into so great an absurdity, as to limit the word *neighbour* to benevolent persons: for nothing is more obvious or certain than that God, in speaking of our neighbours, includes the whole human race" (Calvin, *The Gospels,* AP&A).

Jesus taught us to live by standards higher than those of the scribes (Matt. 5:20). Christ said that instead of hating our enemies, we should love them. He said that instead of cursing those who curse us, we should bless them. Instead of hating those who hate us, we should do good to them. Instead of persecuting those who persecute us, we should pray for them (vs. 44).

Of course, these concepts are as radical today as they were when Jesus delivered the Sermon on the Mount. Putting them into practice is difficult, to say the least. Our Lord never said that following Him would be easy.

Keep in mind that Christ was speaking to individuals and was not attempting to regulate human governments. Even if a nation adopted in principle that it would love its enemies, there would always be those who would refuse to do so. If, however, enough individuals within a nation practiced Christ's teachings, it would revolutionize the character of that nation and how it related to other countries. For the time being, though, we can only anticipate such universal peace, which will be realized only when Christ returns (Isa. 2:1-5; Hos. 2:18; Zech. 9:10; Rev. 11:15).

—*John A. Owston.*

QUESTIONS

1. In what ways did Christ fulfill the law?
2. What was a "jot" and a "tittle" (Matt. 5:18)?
3. What is the meaning of the word "Raca" (vs. 22)?
4. What kind of danger is one in when calling someone a fool?
5. What is the background behind the Greek word translated "hell"?
6. How did Christ strengthen the prohibition against adultery?
7. Why is it wrong to have lustful thoughts and desires?
8. What was the idea behind the "eye for an eye" concept from the Old Testament?
9. Why is it so difficult to turn the other cheek?
10. Why is it not acceptable to hate one's enemies?

—*John A. Owston.*

PRACTICAL POINTS

1. God's Word is more solid and long-lasting than the very ground on which we stand (Matt. 5:17-18).
2. We need to take the sins of anger and hatred much more seriously than we typically do (vss. 21-22).
3. Lust is not a trifle that we can dismiss casually; it can bring us to ruin (vss. 27-28).
4. Jesus calls us to do exactly the opposite of what the world and our own impulses urge us to do (vss. 38-39).
5. Jesus' commands are not just hard; they are impossible without God's help (vss. 43-44).

—Kenneth A. Sponsler.

RESEARCH AND DISCUSSION

1. If Jesus did not abolish the law but upheld it to the smallest detail (Matt. 5:17-18), how is it that we are not "under the law" (Rom. 6:14)?
2. If a believer calls someone a fool, does he lose his salvation and become consigned to hell (Matt. 5:22)? What point was Jesus making?
3. Do you think there is anyone alive (other than Jesus) who has not committed adultery in his heart (vs. 28)? How do we overcome this sin?
4. What are some practical ways that we can turn the other cheek in today's world (vs. 39)?
5. How successful do you think Christians have been at loving their enemies (vs. 44)? How can we improve in this?

—Kenneth A. Sponsler.

Golden Text Illuminated

"Think not that I am come to destroy the law, or the prophets: I am not come to destroy, but to fulfil" (Matthew 5:17).

In what ways did Jesus fulfill the Law and the Prophets? First, we should recognize that God's Law was a reflection of His holiness. As God's Son, Jesus was truly the embodiment of divine perfection. Everything He thought, said, and did was perfectly aligned with God's holiness and truth.

The fact that Jesus did fully obey the Law has extreme implications for our salvation. His perfect obedience provides us with a righteousness that is not our own (I Cor. 1:30; Phil. 3:9). He did all that was necessary to remove the Law's condemnation for everyone with faith in Him (Rom. 10:4; Col. 2:14).

A second way that Christ came to fulfill the Law and Prophets relates to the types and shadows contained in the Old Covenant. The sacrifices and elaborate rituals required by the Mosaic Law truly did not have spiritual meaning in and of themselves (Heb. 10:1). These offered only a rudimentary understanding of spiritual truth, but they are explained fully in the Person of Christ (Col. 2:16-17).

Finally, Jesus fulfilled the messianic prophecies contained in the Law and the Prophets (and the Psalms—Luke 24:44). Jesus is the Prophet whom Moses said would come (Deut. 18:15-18). Jesus is the seed of Abraham through whom all the nations of the world are blessed (Gal. 3:16). He is the Lamb of God who takes away our sins (Isa. 53:6-12; John 1:29).

The reality of Christ fulfilling the Law and the Prophets makes our faith sure and certain.

—Todd Williams.

LESSON 3   JUNE 18, 2023

Scripture Lesson Text

MARK 3:13 And he goeth up into a mountain, and calleth *unto him* whom he would: and they came unto him.

14 And he ordained twelve, that they should be with him, and that he might send them forth to preach,

15 And to have power to heal sicknesses, and to cast out devils:

16 And Simon he surnamed Peter;

17 And James the *son* of Zebedee, and John the brother of James; and he surnamed them Boanerges, which is, The sons of thunder:

18 And Andrew, and Philip, and Bartholomew, and Matthew, and Thomas, and James the *son* of Alphaeus, and Thaddaeus, and Simon the Canaanite,

19 And Judas Iscariot, which also betrayed him: and they went into an house.

6:6 And he went round about the villages, teaching.

7 And he called *unto him* the twelve, and began to send them forth by two and two; and gave them power over unclean spirits;

8 And commanded them that they should take nothing for *their* journey, save a staff only; no scrip, no bread, no money in *their* purse:

9 But *be* shod with sandals; and not put on two coats.

10 And he said unto them, In what place soever ye enter into an house, there abide till ye depart from that place.

11 And whosoever shall not receive you, nor hear you, when ye depart thence, shake off the dust under your feet for a testimony against them. Verily I say unto you, It shall be more tolerable for Sodom and Gomorrha in the day of judgment, than for that city.

12 And they went out, and preached that men should repent.

13 And they cast out many devils, and anointed with oil many that were sick, and healed *them.*

NOTES

A Victorious Kingdom

Lesson Text: Mark 3:13-19; 6:6b-13

Related Scriptures: Matthew 10:1-15; 12:22-32;
Luke 11:14-23; I John 5:14-17

TIME: A.D. 28   PLACES: mountain in Galilee; Galilee

GOLDEN TEXT—"He ordained twelve, that they should be with him, and that he might send them forth to preach" (Mark 3:14).

Lesson Exposition

In Scotland, a young woman began teaching a Sunday school class of poverty-stricken boys. The most unpromising youngster was a boy named Bob. After the first two or three Sundays, he did not return; so the teacher went to look for him. Although the Sunday school superintendent had given Bob some new clothes, they were already worn and dirty when the teacher found him. He was given another new suit, and he came back to Sunday school. But soon he quit again, and the teacher went out once more to find him.

When she did, she discovered that the second set of clothes had gone the way of the first. "I am completely discouraged about Bob," she told the superintendent. They gave Bob a third suit of clothes, and this time he began to attend faithfully. It was not long until he became a Christian.

Who was that obstinate, ragged boy? He was none other than Robert Morrison, who later became the first Protestant missionary to China. He translated the Bible into Chinese and brought the Word of God to millions.

HIS SELECTIONS—Mark 3:13-19

The meeting on the mountain (Mark 3:13). Jesus had reached a moment of tremendous importance: the time when He would choose those who would carry on the ministry He was beginning. They would eventually be the commissioned ones for beginning a worldwide outreach with the gospel.

Luke 6:12 says that before Jesus made His choices, "He went out into a mountain to pray, and continued all night in prayer to God." These appointments were not made without consideration, for the future of the ministry would be resting upon them. At this time Jesus was depending on His Father for the right decisions. Luke 6:13 says Jesus had many disciples but was going to choose from among them those He wanted as His apostles.

The purposes for His choices (Mark 3:14-15). There are two clearly stated purposes for Jesus' choice of these men. The first is "that they should be with him." It was going to take a while for this rough, untrained group to become what Jesus wanted.

Their people skills still needed further honing if they were to be successful in future ministry. The time the apostles spent with Jesus was a time of specific preparation that enabled them to carry His message to the world in the way He wanted it communicated.

Anyone involved in any type of ministry must spend time alone with the Lord before engaging in that ministry.

The second purpose for Jesus' selection of the Twelve was to send them forth to preach, heal, and cast out demons. The Greek word translated "power" in Mark 3:15 means "authority." It would be one thing to preach but quite another to have the ability to heal diseases and cast out demons. Since it is not natural for people to have miraculous power, it was an authority conferred upon them by the Lord.

The first of His disciples (Mark 3:16-17). The first man named in the list of apostles is Simon, whom Jesus "surnamed Peter." This does not mean that He changed his name but rather that He added another name to the one he already had. We often refer to him as Simon Peter.

Peter became a leader of the early church and wrote two epistles that are included in our New Testament. After His resurrection, Jesus made a special personal appearance to Peter, perhaps to encourage and strengthen him after his deep remorse for denying his Lord (Luke 24:34; I Cor. 15:5).

We can read about the initial call of Peter (along with his brother Andrew) and the brothers James and John in Mark 1:16-20. In our present text we learn that Jesus surnamed the latter two "Boanerges" (3:17). This surname apparently was an Aramaic idiom whose literal meaning is "sons of thunder." It is commonly assumed that this nickname gives an insightful indication of their personalities.

The rest of His chosen ones (Mark 3:18-19). There are four lists of the apostles in the New Testament (Matt. 10:2-4; Mark 3:16-19; Luke 6:14-16; Acts 1:13). The Acts list consists of just eleven names, for by then Judas Iscariot was dead and had not yet been replaced. In all four lists, the first four names are the same, though with some change of order. Peter, however, is first in every case.

HIS COMMISSION—Mark 6:6b-13

Sending them out (Mark 6:6b-7). After choosing His disciples, Jesus took them on ministry tours to give them an opportunity to observe how He shared the gospel with others. The time had now arrived for them to go on their own. This ensured that Jesus' ministry was multiplied through these sent-out representatives.

As He sent them forth, Jesus divided the disciples into pairs and commissioned each pair individually as His representatives. It was a common practice for this type of activity to be done by two men rather than one (cf. Deut. 17:6; John 8:17).

The first of Jesus' two purposes in choosing the Twelve was gradually being accomplished: they had been with Him and had learned much. Now the second purpose was being fulfilled: they were being sent out to preach and to have authority to exorcise demons from possessed people. From Mark 3:15, we know they were also given the power to heal diseases. A new phase of Jesus' ministry was about to begin.

Describing their preparation (Mark 6:8-9). In Matthew 10:5-6 we learn that Jesus told the disciples they were to minister specifically to Jewish people on this tour, not to Gentiles or Samaritans. We learn other details from Matthew not included in the Mark account, including exactly what they were to preach and what other ministries they were to perform (vss. 7-8). The next instructions are the same as those in Mark and were given to inform the disciples that they were to totally depend on God for their supplies.

They were to take only one staff, or walking stick, which was a common possession of most people. As far as other provisions were concerned, they were to trust that God would provide for them through the people they ministered to. They were not to take a bag of possessions for their physical needs, nor were they to take food or money.

As for their clothing, they were to wear sandals (which was just ordinary footwear at that time) and to take only the tunic they were wearing. "Coats" (tunics) were knee-length, loosely-fitting inner garments. An extra coat was often used at night as a blanket.

Explaining their approach (Mark 6:10-11). Matthew 10:11 says, "And into whatsoever city or town ye shall enter, enquire who in it is worthy; and there abide till ye go thence." The disciples were to choose carefully where they would reside in each city, and they were to stay in the same place until they moved on. They needed to focus on their ministry instead of moving around looking for other places to stay.

Jesus let them know in advance that they could expect rejection. The instruction He gave about shaking the dust off their feet stemmed from the Jewish practice of shaking the dust off their feet when they left Gentile territory.

This act in essence would show that by rejecting Jesus' disciples, the people were rejecting God and His message to them. This should have provoked serious thought on the part of those watching. It was doubtless the hope of Jesus and His disciples that this might cause some to reconsider and turn to Christ. If they would not, they would face great judgment.

Ministering as commanded (Mark 6:12-13). "They were heralds of the gospel and had repeated success in expelling evil spirits from people. This demonstrated Christ's power over the supernatural world and confirmed His claim to being God" (MacArthur, *The MacArthur Study Bible,* Word).

The message of repentance had been given repeatedly since the days of John the Baptist (Mark 1:4, 14-15). Repentance is a turning from sin to God and is necessary for salvation. It is not a required "work" prior to salvation but rather an evidence of the work of God in one's heart.

—Keith E. Eggert.

QUESTIONS

1. What important decision did Jesus have to make at this time?
2. Why was it so important, and how did He prepare for making it?
3. For what two purposes did Jesus choose the twelve men He did?
4. Why was it so important that the Twelve spend time with Jesus before going out on their own?
5. What special authority did Jesus confer upon these men?
6. Who is named as the first disciple in each list, and what roles did he eventually fill?
7. What took place at the commissioning service Jesus held, and what was the result?
8. What instructions were the disciples given regarding what to take on their mission?
9. How were they to handle rejection when it occurred?
10. What did the men preach, and how did they validate their Master?

—Keith E. Eggert.

PRACTICAL POINTS

1. Spending time with Jesus is a prerequisite for any effective work for Him (Mark 3:13-14).
2. No work we seek to do can be successful without the authority and power of Jesus (Mark 3:15; cf. John 15:5).
3. Trust Christ; He knows you better than anyone else does (Mark 3:16-17; cf. Ps. 139:1-6).
4. Beware! No matter how auspicious the group, betrayers may be present (Mark 3:18-19).
5. Jesus supplies all that is needed for those whom He sends out (6:6*b*-7).
6. We may be sent to preach, but only Christ can change people's lives (vss. 8-13).

—*Don Kakavecos.*

RESEARCH AND DISCUSSION

1. What is the importance of Jesus' initiating the call of the twelve disciples?
2. What do the various personalities of the disciples indicate about the kinds of people God uses? How does this encourage you?
3. Why is spending time with Jesus so crucial to serving Him? In what practical ways can we spend time with Jesus?
4. Should we be surprised when those who seem to be followers of Christ defect? Why or why not (cf. I John 2:19)?
5. Why do you think that Jesus gave the Twelve the directions recorded in Mark 6:8-11? Are they still incumbent upon His followers today? Explain.

—*Don Kakavecos.*

Golden Text Illuminated

"He ordained twelve, that they should be with him, and that he might send them forth to preach" (Mark 3:14).

Jesus chose twelve men. Luke 6:12-13 tells us that He had spent the night on a mountain in prayer, communing with His Father before He made His choices. Jesus habitually spent time alone in prayer seeking His Father's will.

The men Jesus chose would have the important job of carrying the gospel to all the known world. These men would be, in a sense, the creators of the New Testament church. They would also have to endure a time of incredible persecution.

That twelve were chosen is significant. There had been twelve tribes of Israel in the old covenant; now there would be twelve apostles in the new covenant.

The Twelve were more than just friends and followers. Jesus was going to take special time with these twelve men. He was going to teach them all they needed to know so that they could spread the gospel to all the world. In Mark 3:15 we find out that He also gave them power to heal diseases and to cast out demons.

The hope for all of us is this: that ordinary men and women who spend time with Jesus, give themselves totally to God for His service, and are filled with the Holy Spirit can do extraordinary things and change the world! If Jesus has called you into His salvation, you are His disciple. Do great things for Him!

—*Julie Barnhart.*

LESSON 4   JUNE 25, 2023

Scripture Lesson Text

MATT. 13:24 Another parable put he forth unto them, saying, The kingdom of heaven is likened unto a man which sowed good seed in his field:

25 But while men slept, his enemy came and sowed tares among the wheat, and went his way.

26 But when the blade was sprung up, and brought forth fruit, then appeared the tares also.

27 So the servants of the householder came and said unto him, Sir, didst not thou sow good seed in thy field? from whence then hath it tares?

28 He said unto them, An enemy hath done this. The servants said unto him, Wilt thou then that we go and gather them up?

29 But he said, Nay; lest while ye gather up the tares, ye root up also the wheat with them.

30 Let both grow together until the harvest: and in the time of harvest I will say to the reapers, Gather ye together first the tares, and bind them in bundles to burn them: but gather the wheat into my barn.

31 Another parable put he forth unto them, saying, The kingdom of heaven is like to a grain of mustard seed, which a man took, and sowed in his field:

32 Which indeed is the least of all seeds: but when it is grown, it is the greatest among herbs, and becometh a tree, so that the birds of the air come and lodge in the branches thereof.

33 Another parable spake he unto them; The kingdom of heaven is like unto leaven, which a woman took, and hid in three measures of meal, till the whole was leavened.

NOTES

Growing God's Kingdom

Lesson Text: Matthew 13:24-33

Related Scriptures: Daniel 2:24-47; Matthew 13:36-43;
Mark 4:26-32; Luke 13:18-21

TIME: A.D. 28   PLACE: by the Sea of Galilee

GOLDEN TEXT—"Let both grow together until the harvest: and in the time of harvest I will say to the reapers, Gather ye together first the tares, and bind them in bundles to burn them: but gather the wheat into my barn" (Matthew 13:30).

Lesson Exposition

PARABLE OF THE TARES—
Matt. 13:24-30

Good seed (Matt. 13:24). As Matthew 13 opens, the multitude was so large by the Sea of Galilee that Jesus got into a boat and taught the people as they stood on the shore (vss. 1-2). Opening with what has become one of His best-known stories, the parable of the sower, Christ reminded His hearers that not all those who hear come to genuine faith.

After giving and interpreting the parable of the sower (Matt. 13:3-9; 18-23), Jesus proceeded to tell the parable of the tares. All the parables of this chapter are illustrations of Christ's kingdom.

Matthew is the only one of the four Gospels to use the expression "kingdom of heaven." Parallel passages in the other Gospels use the term "kingdom of God." Since Matthew was addressing a largely Jewish readership, he likely avoided the use of God's name, as was customary among the Jews. While there are debates concerning the definitions of "kingdom of heaven" versus "kingdom of God," it is probably best to think in terms of God's rule, whether on earth or in heaven, either in the present or in the future.

As the parable of the sower depicted different soils representing different responses to the gospel, the parable of the tares assures us that Christ alone sows good seed (Matt. 13:37) in the field, which is the world at large. In this case, according to Jesus' own explanation, "the good seed are the children of the kingdom; but the tares are the children of the wicked one" (vs. 38).

Unwanted growth (Matt. 13:25-26). The tares sown by the enemy were actually weeds, probably darnel, which resembles wheat and is not easily detected at first. "We must beware of Satan's counterfeits. He has counterfeit Christians (2 Cor. 11:26) who believe a counterfeit Gospel (Gal. 1:6-9). He encourages a counterfeit righteousness (Rom. 10:1-3), and even has a counterfeit church (Rev. 2:9). At the end of the age, he will produce a counterfeit Christ (2 Thess. 2:1-12)" (Wiersbe, *The Bible Exposition Commentary,* Cook).

The enemy sowed the tares at night, which is typical of Satan's strategy. His work is mostly covert, and by the time it becomes evident that he is behind an evil deed, the damage has already occurred and reversing the consequences of his work is difficult, if not impossible.

As we have noted, Jesus identified the tares as the children of the evil one. They are false Christians. "Satan cannot uproot the plants (true Christians), so he plants counterfeit Christians in their midst. In this parable, the good seed is not the Word of God. It represents people converted through trusting the Word. The field is not human hearts; the field is the world. Christ is sowing true believers in various places that they might bear fruit (John 12:23-26). But, wherever Christ sows a true Christian, Satan comes and sows a counterfeit" (Wiersbe).

Overreaction (Matt. 13:27-28). Discovering that tares had been sown among the wheat, the servants of the owner approached him concerning the seed he had sown in his field. Assuming good seed had been sown, the servants asked an obvious question: "Whence then hath it tares?"

Knowing that good seed had originally been sown in his field, the owner realized that some enemy was responsible.

Since the tares represented a danger to the entire crop, the servants suggested that they quickly uproot the tares that had been sown. While this might seem a reasonable suggestion, it could actually have done more harm than good.

You can probably imagine similar situations in both families and churches in which quick action might result in more harm than good. This, of course, does not mean we should be content to allow evil to flourish in our world. But forcibly trying to uproot evil can sometimes be counterproductive to the ultimate goals of the gospel.

Wise counsel (Matt. 13:29-30). The owner wisely told his servants that in trying to rid the field of the tares, the wheat would likely be endangered. Until harvesttime, when the two were more easily distinguished, the wheat and tares were to be permitted to grow side by side in the field. At that time, the tares could be gathered and burned and the wheat stored in the farmer's barn.

As Jesus later interpreted the parable, both the wheat and the tares, that is, both the righteous and the wicked, will continue to the end of the age. At that time, judgment will fall on the wicked (Matt. 13:39-43). As for the righteous, they will be rewarded by the Father. Scripture affirms over and over that judgment is coming (cf. II Thess. 1:7-9; II Pet. 3:10-13; Rev. 20:11-15).

PARABLE OF THE MUSTARD SEED—Matt. 13:31-32

Small seed (Matt. 13:31). Once again, the purpose of the parable was to illustrate something about the kingdom of heaven. In this case, God's kingdom "is like to a grain of mustard seed" (vs. 31). Other ancient Jewish literature indicates that the mustard seed was frequently used proverbially.

Large tree (Matt. 13:32). Technically, there are other seeds smaller than the mustard seed, but such seeds were unknown to people in that part of the world. In spite of its small beginnings, the mustard seed grew to become the "greatest among herbs" and could even be described as a tree.

Whether there is any significance to the birds in the parable is uncertain. This could just be coloring in the parable, that is, something that enhances the total word picture Christ was painting without having any particular interpretative significance.

On the other hand, there are some passages in the Old Testament in which such imagery did have significance. In Ezekiel 31, the Assyrians were described as a cedar of Lebanon (vs. 3) with many birds and beasts finding shelter therein (vs. 6). This presumably refers to people, not animals. A similar passage is found in Daniel 4. In this case, King Nebuchadnezzar had a dream of a large tree with abundant fruit. Birds of the air also dwelled in its branches (vss. 10-12). Interpreted by Daniel (vss. 19-22), the tree represented the king and his worldwide dominion. The birds represented nations.

Consequently, the birds in the Lord's parable may in fact depict both the preaching of the gospel to all nations (Matt. 28:19-20; Mark 16:15-16) and the eventual conquest by Christ's kingdom.

Although the beginnings of Christ's kingdom appear to be small and insignificant, like the mustard seed, it is destined for greatness and glory. The fact that the Jews of Jesus' day rejected Him (John 1:10-11) does not mean that the plans and purposes of God are forever thwarted (Rom. 11:1-5). Gentiles have been grafted into the natural tree (vs. 17), enjoying the privileges promised to Israel.

PARABLE OF THE LEAVEN—
Matt. 13:33

In some ways, the meaning of the parable of the mustard seed and the parable of the leaven is the same. The two parables might be summarized with the phrase "small beginnings; great results." There are, however, some differences between them.

Regarding the mustard seed, once planted, the growth would be evident. The seed, in fact, germinates quickly and grows rapidly. The kingdom's growth would be visible to all.

In the case of leaven, or yeast, the work is hidden. Of course, in time the work of the yeast does become evident as the dough rises. "If there is a distinction between this parable and the last one, it is that the mustard seed suggests extensive growth and the yeast intensive transformation" (Barker and Kohlenberger, eds., *The Expositor's Bible Commentary, Abridged*, Zondervan).

—John Alva Owston.

QUESTIONS

1. What preceded the parable of the tares?
2. Are "kingdom of heaven" and "kingdom of God" the same or different? Explain.
3. What are some differences between the parable of the sower and the parable of the tares?
4. What were tares? How did they get into the field in Jesus' parable?
5. What do the tares represent? Where might we see tares today?
6. What dangers were involved in uprooting the tares? How can this be applied today?
7. What point was Jesus making with the parable of the tares?
8. What interpretations have been given concerning the birds in the mustard plant?
9. What was the main point of the parable of the mustard seed?
10. How is the parable of the leaven both different from and similar to the mustard seed parable?

—John Alva Owston.

PRACTICAL POINTS

1. Sometimes our enemies do everything they can to ruin our good work (Matt. 13:24-26).
2. It is important to seek counsel rather than to rush forward and make hasty decisions (vs. 27).
3. Choosing to wait rather than immediately reacting is a sign of wisdom (vss. 28-29).
4. At the appointed time, those who do not belong to God will be permanently separated from those who do (vs. 30).
5. God can cause those who seem insignificant to become people of importance (vss. 31-32).
6. Seemingly small acts can have enormous results (vs. 33).

—Charity G. Carter.

RESEARCH AND DISCUSSION

1. What are some modern-day examples of good seed that people of God sow (Matt. 13:24)?
2. Why were the men not punished for the growth of tares (vs. 25)? Does neglect enable the enemy to plant weeds among the crops?
3. Why did the owner of the crops not seem surprised when he learned of the maliciousness (vss. 27-30)?
4. What should we do when we think we discern that someone is not a genuine Christian (a tare among the wheat)?
5. In what ways do people find shelter in the kingdom of God (vss. 31-32)? Are all such people necessarily genuine believers?

—Charity G. Carter.

Golden Text Illuminated

"Let both grow together until the harvest: and in the time of harvest I will say to the reapers, Gather ye together first the tares, and bind them in bundles to burn them: but gather the wheat into my barn" (Matthew 13:30).

Some organic farmers have begun "flame weeding" their cornfields. A tractor pulls an implement that shoots flames along the ground through rows of knee-high corn. It withers the weeds without harming the crop. In today's parable, Jesus also speaks of burning up weeds, but this happens only at the harvest. Rather than immediately eradicating the tares from His crop, the Lord deems it better to let them grow up among the wheat. This is a truly remarkable teaching, since it signals Jesus' intention to let evil people remain in the world along with His true children.

So why does God let the tares remain? Because the uprooting of evildoers involves judgment upon the world. If God were to visit His righteous judgment on the world before believers have matured and borne their fruit, God's purpose and plan would be thwarted by His own judgment. God's wisdom therefore dictates that He forestall any such judgment on the world until the full measure of His elect is complete. Then both the wicked and the righteous can be uprooted from the world without harming God's plan. The righteous will then be gathered in safely, and the wicked will be judged.

Praise God for His great and wise plan that resolves all things justly and with finality!

—Todd Williams.

LESSON 5   JULY 2, 2023

Scripture Lesson Text

LUKE 11:1 And it came to pass, that, as he was praying in a certain place, when he ceased, one of his disciples said unto him, Lord, teach us to pray, as John also taught his disciples.

2 And he said unto them, When ye pray, say, Our Father which art in heaven, Hallowed be thy name. Thy kingdom come. Thy will be done, as in heaven, so in earth.

3 Give us day by day our daily bread.

4 And forgive us our sins; for we also forgive every one that is indebted to us. And lead us not into temptation; but deliver us from evil.

5 And he said unto them, Which of you shall have a friend, and shall go unto him at midnight, and say unto him, Friend, lend me three loaves;

6 For a friend of mine in his journey is come to me, and I have nothing to set before him?

7 And he from within shall answer and say, Trouble me not: the door is now shut, and my children are with me in bed; I cannot rise and give thee.

8 I say unto you, Though he will not rise and give him, because he is his friend, yet because of his importunity he will rise and give him as many as he needeth.

9 And I say unto you, Ask, and it shall be given you; seek, and ye shall find; knock, and it shall be opened unto you.

10 For every one that asketh receiveth; and he that seeketh findeth; and to him that knocketh it shall be opened.

11 If a son shall ask bread of any of you that is a father, will he give him a stone? or if *he ask* a fish, will he for a fish give him a serpent?

12 Or if he shall ask an egg, will he offer him a scorpion?

13 If ye then, being evil, know how to give good gifts unto your children: how much more shall *your* heavenly Father give the Holy Spirit to them that ask him?

NOTES

Praying to God

Lesson Text: Luke 11:1-13

Related Scriptures: Exodus 16:15-22; Matthew 6:5-15; Romans 8:14-17, 26-27; I John 1:5-10

TIME: A.D. 29   PLACE: Judea

GOLDEN TEXT—"When ye pray, say, Our Father which art in heaven, Hallowed be thy name. Thy kingdom come. Thy will be done, as in heaven, so in earth" (Luke 11:2).

Lesson Exposition

NEED FOR PRAYER—Luke 11:1

After watching Jesus pray somewhere, one of the Lord's disciples asked Him to teach them to pray. Jesus' prayers made the disciples aware of their own inadequacies when it came to prayer.

The disciples also knew that John the Baptist had taught his disciples to pray, and they likewise wanted Jesus to teach them on this vital subject.

PATTERN FOR PRAYER—
Luke 11:2-4

Worshipping God (Luke 11:2a). In responding to His disciple's question, Jesus presented what is commonly called the Lord's Prayer. As such, it is a model for our prayers.

When we pray, we are to acknowledge God as our Father. This is not a form of address commonly used in the Old Testament, but with Jesus it becomes the standard way of addressing God.

The title "Father" suggests relationship. God is not unknowable. We can relate to Him in a personal way. Indeed, only those who know Him personally can address God in this way.

All prayer should involve worship, and worship means recognizing the unique character and attributes of God. Not only is God to be addressed as our Father, but He is also to be acknowledged as transcendent and sovereign. We are to embrace both of these truths.

So in praying, God is to be acknowledged as perfectly holy. "Hallowed" means "treated as holy." "Name" speaks of the Person and character of God. Thus, in prayer we are to worship God as the Holy One.

Desiring God's will (Luke 11:2b). Prayer involves praise and worship, but it also involves petition—asking God for things. Particularly, Jesus said we are to ask for God's will to be done. This is to be our highest desire, and it precedes all other requests.

Our desire and prayer must be that God's desire will be accomplished on earth as it is in heaven. While it is to be our prayer that this will be done in any given situation right now, we recognize that His will shall be fully manifested on this earth only when Christ comes again, this time in majesty and power.

We thus should be praying for Christ to return (cf. Rev. 22:20). Our time here on earth is to be an active cooperation with God to prayerfully hasten Christ's return (II Pet. 3:12). We are to pray for His return because of our desire to see His will perfectly fulfilled.

Making our requests (Luke 11:3). Jesus' model prayer also instructs us to ask God to meet our physical needs. "Bread" stands for all food and here suggests more broadly all the physical and material provisions we need for daily life.

Such a prayer for God's daily provision might seem irrelevant to people who never lack such things. However, to pray this way is to acknowledge our dependence upon the Lord for everything we have.

Seeking forgiveness (Luke 11:4). Prayer also involves asking God to meet our spiritual needs. This is a model prayer for God's children, those who can call Him "Father." Thus, this request does not involve salvation, but rather our relationship with the Father. Daily sins require daily forgiveness to restore us to a position of communion with God.

Our sins are viewed as debts. They are debts that cannot be paid off; they must be forgiven.

God's forgiveness of us is tied to our forgiveness of others—those who are in our debt. This does not mean that we earn God's forgiveness by forgiving others, for God's forgiveness is by grace. But if we refuse to forgive others, we are in fact sinning ourselves and cannot be in a right relationship with God (cf. Col. 3:13).

The final petition set forth in Jesus' model prayer is "Lead us not into temptation; but deliver us from evil" (Luke 11:4). This request is difficult to understand.

It is probably best to take this request as a "plea that God, in his providence, will spare the supplicant from needless temptations" (Pfeiffer and Harrison, eds., *The Wycliffe Bible Commentary,* Moody). Our words and actions sometimes put us in situations where temptation can overwhelm us. We are to pray that God will spare us from this.

"Evil" in Luke 11:4 is almost certainly a reference to Satan, the evil one. We are to pray that God will spare us from the devil, that is, deliver us out of his hands.

The Lord's Prayer is not a prayer Jesus would pray Himself, for He did not need forgiveness. Rather, He offered this prayer as a model for us. It is not a prayer we need to repeat endlessly but one that should be reflected in our own personal prayers. We are to recognize God for who He is, we are to recognize His will as supreme, and we are to recognize Him as the true source to meet our physical and spiritual needs.

PERSISTENCE IN PRAYER—
Luke 11:5-8

Simple request (Luke 11:5-6). Jesus not only taught the disciples how to pray; He also encouraged them to pray and to pray with persistence. He did so through a parable.

Jesus told of a man who was unprepared for a guest who arrived unexpectedly late at night. Travelers had few options for lodging and were seldom able to alert friends in advance of their arrival.

Hospitality was a sacred duty, and people depended on one another for lodging while traveling. They tried to be ready for unexpected guests, but Jesus described a man who was unprepared and had no food for his late-arriving friend. So he went to a neighbor and asked for three loaves of bread.

Repeated request (Luke 11:7-8). The friend was reluctant to get out of bed and give his neighbor the loaves he requested. It was an inconvenience to get up and disturb the whole family, who slept together in a one-room house. Jesus noted, however, that the man in bed would finally grant the request because of his friend's persistence in asking for the bread.

The parable has one simple point: persistence pays off. Even an earthly friend will extend help to us when we persistently seek it.

FOUNDATION FOR PRAYER—
Luke 11:9-13

A habitual practice (Luke 11:9-10). These verses contain the application of Jesus' parable. "Ask" is a term that describes a humble request of a superior. "Seek" adds the idea of effort, and "knock" adds the thought of repetition, since one never knocks only once. In fact, the tenses of all the verbs indicate persistence.

Verse 10 repeats the statements of verse 9 but adds that everyone who persistently prays in this way will be satisfied.

An earthly illustration (Luke 11:11-12). Here Jesus drew a contrast between people and God—a contrast that is implied in His previous parable (vss. 5-8). He said that fathers will surely give their children good things when they ask for them.

A loving Father (Luke 11:13). Jesus' argument was from the lesser to the greater. If earthly fathers—who are sinners (cf. Matt. 7:11)—desire to give the best to their children, how much more will God give good things to His children? He does this not because He is annoyed by our requests but because He is our loving Heavenly Father.

While the parallel passage in Matthew 7 speaks of God giving "good gifts," here the greatest gift, the Holy Spirit, is the good thing God gives. The Spirit's power is in view here. This is what we need in every situation that calls for prayer.

The point of Jesus' teaching is that God is willing to answer our prayers. Persistence is important and needed, but the reason we are to be persistent in prayer is that God is always willing to answer.

But why be persistent if God knows our needs and is willing to answer? The purpose of persistent prayer is not to convince God or to wear down His resistance. Rather, it is for our sake. Persistence reveals to us the true nature of our prayers. Sometimes we are not persistent because we are not very serious.

God is not a vending machine that automatically gives us what we want when we insert the right prayer. He is a person, and if we want His will and His best, we must approach Him with earnest faith and persistence.

—*Jarl K. Waggoner.*

QUESTIONS

1. Why did the disciple want Jesus to teach them all how to pray?
2. What is suggested by addressing God as "our Father" (Luke 11:2)?
3. What does "hallowed" mean? How do we hallow God's name?
4. What request in Jesus' model prayer precedes all others?
5. What should motivate us to pray for Christ's imminent return?
6. In what way is God's forgiveness of us tied to our forgiveness of others?
7. What is meant by the plea to "lead us not into temptation" (vs. 4)?
8. What point was Jesus' parable teaching?
9. What promise is given to one who is persistent in prayer?
10. How did Jesus underscore God's willingness to answer prayer?

—*Jarl K. Waggoner.*

PRACTICAL POINTS

1. Like the disciples, we should look to Jesus' model of prayer (Luke 11:1).
2. We should start our prayers by giving reverence to God (vs. 2).
3. When we pray, we should ask God to provide for our needs (vs. 3).
4. Even though we know God will forgive us, we should pray for the strength to not sin (vs. 4).
5. We need to stay persistent in prayer, even when God has not yet answered our prayers (vss. 5-8).
6. Everyone who truly seeks God will find God (vss. 9-10).
7. If people can give good gifts, we can trust God to give us what is good for us (vss. 11-13).

—Stuart Olley.

RESEARCH AND DISCUSSION

1. Why did Jesus go to certain places to pray (Luke 11:1; cf. 6:12; 9:18)? How could doing that help us in our prayers?
2. What practical steps do you see in Jesus' example of prayer (Luke 11:2-4; cf. Matt. 6:9-13)?
3. What are the similarities between Jesus' example of the friend asking for bread and the parable of the persistent widow (Luke 11:5-8; cf. 18:1-8)?
4. How can obeying Jesus by being steadfast in prayer help us be more like Him (Luke 11:8; cf. II Pet. 1:5-11)?
5. What are the good things we should ask God for (Luke 11:11-13; cf. Jas. 1:5, 17)?

—Stuart Olley.

Golden Text Illuminated

"When ye pray, say, Our Father which art in heaven, Hallowed be thy name. Thy kingdom come. Thy will be done, as in heaven, so in earth" (Luke 11:2).

"Our Father." This is a perfect beginning that reminds us of several beautiful, reassuring truths.

1. God is Father, not some vague, aloof deity. We are His family.
2. God is our God, not merely a deity we have heard of who belongs to others but not to us.
3. How beautiful that of all the titles that are rightfully His, the one He wants us to use is the most intimate and loving.

"Which art in heaven." In this we not only recognize His high position of authority but also confess that He is separate from this sinful, sorrow-filled world.

"Hallowed be thy name." We confess that God's name is holy to us and that our desire is for everyone to regard His name as holy.

"Thy kingdom come." In this phrase we look to the future with hope. His kingdom is coming!

"Thy will be done." If we truly believe that He loves us and wants what is best for us, we can say this phrase with confidence.

"As in heaven, so in earth." For us to pray for God's will to be done on earth requires not just a willing heart but obedience as well. Jesus' model prayer displays both the depth of God's wisdom and the humility and simplicity of a true disciple.

—Kimberly Rae.

Scripture Lesson Text

LUKE 14:7 And he put forth a parable to those which were bidden, when he marked how they chose out the chief rooms; saying unto them,

8 When thou art bidden of any *man* to a wedding, sit not down in the highest room; lest a more honourable man than thou be bidden of him;

9 And he that bade thee and him come and say to thee, Give this man place; and thou begin with shame to take the lowest room.

10 But when thou art bidden, go and sit down in the lowest room; that when he that bade thee cometh, he may say unto thee, Friend, go up higher: then shalt thou have worship in the presence of them that sit at meat with thee.

11 For whosoever exalteth himself shall be abased; and he that humbleth himself shall be exalted.

15 And when one of them that sat at meat with him heard these things, he said unto him, Blessed *is* he that shall eat bread in the kingdom of God.

16 Then said he unto him, A certain man made a great supper, and bade many:

17 And sent his servant at supper time to say to them that were bidden, Come; for all things are now ready.

18 And they all with one *consent* began to make excuse. The first said unto him, I have bought a piece of ground, and I must needs go and see it: I pray thee have me excused.

19 And another said, I have bought five yoke of oxen, and I go to prove them: I pray thee have me excused.

20 And another said, I have married a wife, and therefore I cannot come.

21 So that servant came, and shewed his lord these things. Then the master of the house being angry said to his servant, Go out quickly into the streets and lanes of the city, and bring in hither the poor, and the maimed, and the halt, and the blind.

22 And the servant said, Lord, it is done as thou hast commanded, and yet there is room.

23 And the lord said unto the servant, Go out into the highways and hedges, and compel *them* to come in, that my house may be filled.

24 For I say unto you, That none of those men which were bidden shall taste of my supper.

NOTES

Accept God's Invitation!

Lesson Text Luke 14:7-11, 15-24

Related Scriptures: Proverbs 25:6-7; Matthew 21:42-44; 22:1-14

TIME: A.D. 30   PLACE: Perea

GOLDEN TEXT—"And the lord said unto the servant, Go out into the highways and hedges, and compel them to come in, that my house may be filled" (Luke 14:23).

Lesson Exposition

The events recorded in Luke 14 took place at a banquet on the Sabbath Day in the home of one of the chief Pharisees (vs. 1).

ATTITUDES—Luke 14:7-11

An observation (Luke 14:7). Jesus had already observed that the people at the banquet had been acting to promote themselves. As they entered the room, they had been scrambling for the places of honor at the banquet table. The most honored places were those closest to the host.

A wrong choice (Luke 14:8-9). Although Jesus was probably not at a wedding feast Himself, He used that as His illustration. He said that when a person was invited to a wedding feast, he should not assume that he should go to the best seat, for the host might have invited someone more deserving of that seat. When that guest arrived, the host would come to the first arrival and ask him to move to another seat farther away; this would prove to be a most embarrassing moment.

A right choice (Luke 14:10-11). Jesus said that one should go to the lowest place instead of the highest. If the host wants him to be in an honored position, he will come and invite the guest to sit in the better seat. In the process it will be publicly seen that he deserves special recognition. Instead of being embarrassed, he will be properly exalted before the other attendees.

Jesus then verbalized a very important life principle: "Whosoever exalteth himself shall be abased; and he that humbleth himself shall be exalted" (vs. 11). The attitude of the world is to promote oneself and achieve recognition in order to be successful. God's desire is that we humble ourselves and let Him do the exalting if and whenever He sees fit. Self-exaltation will ultimately result in humiliation.

In the wedding feast situation, it was not the one who honored himself who was truly honored but the one the host honored. Jesus was saying that it is not the one who exalts himself who is truly honored but rather the one whom God exalts. As God's children, it is far better to humbly carry out whatever ministry He has allowed us and not seek public acclaim. When we endeavor to exalt ourselves, we usually look foolish; but when God honors us in some way, we become a testimony to others of how He can use us effectively.

OPPORTUNITIES—Luke 14:15-20

Blessing (Luke 14:15). Jesus followed His teaching on humility with a teaching directed to those who host dinners (vss. 12-14). He told them that they should not limit their invitations to those who have the ability to reciprocate but should include those who are financially unable to do so. For this they would be blessed and rewarded by God Himself at the resurrection. It was upon hearing this instruction that someone present spoke up with a pronouncement of blessing of his own.

This particular guest did not understand what Jesus had been teaching, and his statement sounds like a pious expression meant to impress Jesus. He seems to have connected in his mind the idea of being honored and blessed at this present feast with their presumed enjoyment of the feast in the kingdom of God. He was carried away by the occasion. There is a hint in his statement that he assumed every outwardly righteous Jew would automatically be welcomed into the kingdom.

Such an understanding leads us to think that this man was one of the Pharisees. When Jesus mentioned the resurrection of the just (vs. 14), this man's mind went to earthly glory. It may have been his understanding that when the Messiah came, He would deliver the Jews from the domination of the Roman Empire. Then they would live in peace and prosperity, without warfare and uncertainty.

Invitations (Luke 14:16-17). In this parable Jesus used the idea of a great supper to portray salvation, which results, of course, in becoming a part of God's kingdom. The invitations to the supper represent the invitation God has given to people to become part of His family through His Son, Jesus. Since it was clear to Jesus that the man who had just spoken did not understand salvation, He specifically addressed him in response to his comment about eating in the kingdom.

In Jesus' parable a certain man planned a huge dinner party and sent invitations to everyone he wanted to attend. It was customary to invite people well in advance of the event, with an approximate starting time specified. When everything was ready, a servant went to tell those who had accepted the invitation that it was time for them to come. Apparently, everyone had accepted the invitation, so the plans had been made accordingly. At this point it would be extremely insulting to not show up for the event.

Throughout the Old Testament, announcements were made that the Messiah was coming and that the Jews should be getting ready for His arrival. The announcements were received and accepted gladly. No one knew the exact time of His arrival, but it was certainly good news that He was coming, for He would provide deliverance for His people.

Excuses (Luke 14:18-20). As the servant went from person to person to let them know it was time for the dinner to begin, he received many excuses as to why they could not attend after all. Every excuse reeked of insincerity. Each person indicated a preoccupation with other things that he considered more important than the dinner. The first said he had bought a piece of ground and needed to go see it. The second said he had bought five yoke of oxen and needed to test them. The third said he could not come because he had just married.

It is easy to see these are nothing more than excuses. The people's preoccupation with things they felt were more important reveals a lack of interest in fulfilling the commitment they had made when they accepted the initial invitation.

When the Messiah finally arrived in

Israel, a large number of the people were so involved with their everyday lives that they were not interested in hearing what He had to say. They paid little or no attention to the message He proclaimed.

DECISIONS—Luke 14:21-24

New invitations (Luke 14:21-22). When the servant returned and told his master about the excuses he had received, the master became angry and devised another plan. The dinner was ready, and time was now of the essence. If those invited were so unappreciative that they would offer terribly lame excuses for not coming, invitations would go to those who would respond eagerly and be grateful for them.

The master specified that the servant should go into the various areas of the city, both the broad streets and the narrow lanes, and invite the poor, maimed (crippled), halt (lame), and blind. The master had first invited those considered of a higher class, but he now turned to others when his invitation was rejected. In the eyes of the Pharisees, these people were outcasts, much like the tax collectors.

In Israel it was the religious leaders who first rejected Jesus and eventually saw to His death. They had an opportunity to receive Him but refused. Jesus therefore turned to the common people with His invitation. Since the religious leaders showed no interest in spiritual truth, Jesus went directly to the people with His teaching.

In Jesus' parable, the servant reported to his master that he had done as he was told. The people had responded and come, but there was still room left for many more.

Expansion and exclusions (Luke 14:23-24). Since there was still room in the dining hall, the master told his servant to expand the parameters of the invitation. Now he should go beyond the city limits out into the countryside and invite people on the highways or along the hedges that acted as fences. He was to speak urgently to them, compelling them to come so that the master's house would be full of people.

The master's concluding statement was a somber one: "For I say unto you, That none of those men which were bidden shall taste of my supper" (vs. 24). Those who had rejected his invitation would be excluded forever. Jesus' parable described His own offer of salvation for people to become part of the family of God. It remains true today that many reject the invitation while others accept it gladly.
—*Keith E. Eggert.*

QUESTIONS

1. What had Jesus observed as He watched the people coming in?
2. How did Jesus say they should act when attending such an event?
3. What principle did Jesus set forth regarding being exalted?
4. What lesson about self-exaltation can we learn from this?
5. What statement did one of the guests make to Jesus after this?
6. What was his understanding concerning the kingdom of heaven?
7. How did Jesus portray salvation in His parable in response to the guest's statement?
8. What happened to the master in Jesus' parable after he invited a large group of guests to dinner?
9. What steps did he then take to fill his banquet hall with people, and who responded?
10. How are many people today much like the Israelites of Jesus' day in their response to Him?

—*Keith E. Eggert.*

PRACTICAL POINTS

1. God honors those who do not seek honors from people (Luke 14:7-11).
2. God has chosen to use us as His ambassadors to invite the lost to salvation (vss. 15-17).
3. We should not be surprised if the gospel is met with excuses rather than joyous acceptance (vss. 18-20).
4. The despised and forgotten of the world are the objects of God's love (vss. 21-22).
5. We should make every effort to take the gospel to unbelievers, but ultimately they are responsible for how they respond (vss. 23-24).

—Jarl K. Waggoner.

RESEARCH AND DISCUSSION

1. How do you think Jesus would evaluate some of our social customs (Luke 14:8-11)?
2. How can we consciously develop a humble attitude without seeming self-righteous (vss. 10-11)?
3. How can people who are so mistaken about their own destiny be so sure of their acceptance by God (vs. 15)?
4. Why do people feel the need to offer excuses for rejecting Christ (vss. 18-20)?
5. What is the Christian's responsibility in bringing people to Christ (Luke 14:23; cf. 24:46-47; John 6:44)? Is there a sense in which we should "compel" people?
6. What aspects of God's character are revealed by the statements of the master in Luke 14:23-24?

—Jarl K. Waggoner.

Golden Text Illuminated

"And the lord said unto the servant, Go out into the highways and hedges, and compel them to come in, that my house may be filled" (Luke 14:23).

Kindness and generosity naturally inspire gratefulness. There is something wrong with a person who responds to graciousness with coldness. Sadly, this latter reaction came from every guest the rich man had invited to his banquet in Jesus' parable.

This wealthy banquet host beautifully illustrates the abundant grace of God. Let us consider how this is true.

First, the host did not simply put up a sign offering to feed any passersby. He sent his servant out to *compel* people to come in. We see that is similar to God's behavior. As John 3:16 tells us, He sent His Son to the world to convince people to accept His kindness and mercy. At first, it might seem odd that people actually need any convincing. Are they not being offered a free pardon for all their sins? Yes, it seems that people should all jump at the opportunity! But Scripture makes us face reality: there are none who seek God (Rom. 3:11).

Second, note where the servant in the parable was sent: to the "highways and hedges." This indicates that the new group of guests would likely be common people and possibly poor.

Finally, why was the banquet host so willing to invite common people and poor people to enjoy his feast? Because he wanted a full house. He was not stingy. Like God, he was so gracious that he wanted as many as possible to enjoy his lavish abundance.

—Todd Williams.

LESSON 7   JULY 16, 2023

Scripture Lesson Text

LUKE 16:19 There was a certain rich man, which was clothed in purple and fine linen, and fared sumptuously every day:

20 And there was a certain beggar named Lazarus, which was laid at his gate, full of sores,

21 And desiring to be fed with the crumbs which fell from the rich man's table: moreover the dogs came and licked his sores.

22 And it came to pass, that the beggar died, and was carried by the angels into Abraham's bosom: the rich man also died, and was buried;

23 And in hell he lift up his eyes, being in torments, and seeth Abraham afar off, and Lazarus in his bosom.

24 And he cried and said, Father Abraham, have mercy on me, and send Lazarus, that he may dip the tip of his finger in water, and cool my tongue; for I am tormented in this flame.

25 But Abraham said, Son, remember that thou in thy lifetime receivedst thy good things, and likewise Lazarus evil things: but now he is comforted, and thou art tormented.

26 And beside all this, between us and you there is a great gulf fixed: so that they which would pass from hence to you cannot; neither can they pass to us, that *would come* from thence.

27 Then he said, I pray thee therefore, father, that thou wouldest send him to my father's house:

28 For I have five brethren; that he may testify unto them, lest they also come into this place of torment.

29 Abraham saith unto him, They have Moses and the prophets; let them hear them.

30 And he said, Nay, father Abraham: but if one went unto them from the dead, they will repent.

31 And he said unto him, If they hear not Moses and the prophets, neither will they be persuaded, though one rose from the dead.

A Warning for the Hard-Hearted

Lesson Text: Luke 16:19-31

Related Scriptures: Matthew 6:19-20;
Hebrews 3:7-19; Revelation 20:11-15; 21:5-8

TIME: A.D. 30   PLACE: probably Perea

GOLDEN TEXT—"Son, remember that thou in thy lifetime receivedst thy good things, and likewise Lazarus evil things: but now he is comforted, and thou art tormented" (Luke 16:25).

Lesson Exposition

RICH MAN, POOR MAN—
Luke 16:19-21

Prosperity (Luke 16:19). Though unnamed, the "certain rich man" in this story is often referred to as Dives. The supposed name derives from the Latin Vulgate version of the Bible, as the Latin word for "rich" is *dives*. This, however, was not a personal name. In one line, the rich man is described in such a way that there is no doubt concerning his luxurious lifestyle. To be "clothed in purple" meant that he wore the clothing of royalty, though there is nothing to indicate that he occupied an official government post. Likewise, the "fine linen," imported from the Nile River valley, was another sign of wealth. In addition, the rich man "fared sumptuously every day"—he feasted on the finest food in great abundance. He would no doubt have been the envy of many people.

One of the questions often asked concerning our lesson text concerns the nature of the story itself. Is it a parable or the recounting of actual events? Most would refer to it as a parable, but that in no way diminishes the truth it conveys.

Poverty (Luke 16:20-21). "Lazarus" was a rather common name in New Testament times (cf. John 11:1-44). Significantly, the name Lazarus means "he whom God has helped." This is appropriate, as Lazarus was not aided by the rich man but by God Himself.

To be placed where many people passed by, including by the gate of a wealthy man's property, was common for beggars in biblical times (cf. Mark 10:46; Acts 3:1-2). That Lazarus was "laid at his gate" (Luke 16:20) indicates a lack of mobility. Being "full of sores" reveals a condition both painful and likely infectious. The mental image we draw from this brief description certainly elicits sympathy for this man's plight.

Lazarus was not asking to be admitted to the rich man's house to be seated with him at his fine table. All he wanted was the meager leftovers from the rich man's feasts—the scraps.

REWARD AND RETRIBUTION—Luke 16:22-23

Heaven (Luke 16:22). As will happen to all of us, both Lazarus and the rich man died. Carried by the angels, Lazarus was escorted into the presence of Abraham to rest at his side. Being the father of the Hebrew people, Abraham was seen as the overseer of paradise, the place to which the righteous go after death (23:43). To be with Abraham meant that Lazarus was with the patriarchs of Israel (13:28). The picture is of a great banquet enjoyed by all the redeemed. Lazarus would not have to beg for food any longer. Whether paradise and heaven were seen as identical at this time is unclear. Paul seemed to use these words interchangeably (cf. II Cor. 12:1-4).

That Lazarus was taken to paradise certainly indicates that he was a righteous man, although nothing is stated about his faith or character. He was not, however, taken to paradise simply because he was poor. There are poor people who are very evil, and there are rich people who are very godly. "Lazarus was righteous not because he was poor but because he depended on God" (Walvoord and Zuck, eds., *The Bible Knowledge Commentary,* Cook). That being said, riches do present temptations never imagined by the poor. Generally speaking, Scripture depicts God as being on the side of the poor when they face oppression from the rich (cf. Jas. 2:5-7; 5:1-6).

Hell (Luke 16:23). In direct contrast to Lazarus, the rich man went to hell. The word translated "hell" in our text is the Greek *hades,* which was understood as the world of the dead and equivalent to the Hebrew *sheol,* often found in the Old Testament. As understood by many in antiquity, hades was not necessarily a place of suffering but just the place people went after death. However, in the New Testament, hades is usually depicted as a place of torment (cf. Luke 10:15; Rev. 1:18; 6:8; 20:13-14).

As the rich man closed his eyes in death, he immediately opened them in torment. Not only could he see where he was, but he could also see where Lazarus was! Whether this means the lost can see what they have missed is an open question. If so, it will add to their mental anguish as they view the bliss of the saved.

REQUEST DENIED—Luke 16:24-28

Great anguish (Luke 16:24). Realizing where he was caused the rich man to cry out for mercy. As a Jew, it was appropriate for him to address Abraham as "Father." But physical descent from Abraham was no guarantee of being in a correct spiritual relationship with God (cf. 3:7-9; 13:28-30).

Since the rich man was able to see Lazarus being comforted, he pleaded with the patriarch to send the former beggar to his aid. His request was simple. He wanted Lazarus to dip the tip of his finger in some water and cool his tongue with a few drops.

Great gulf (Luke 16:25-26). In reply to his plea for Lazarus to help alleviate his pain, Abraham reminded the rich man of his former life of luxury. To be sure, if we go to hell, we take our memories with us. But the memories of a life of ease would only serve to increase the mental anguish experienced by the rich man. That Lazarus by contrast received "evil things" simply means he received bad things—namely, poverty, privation, and pain. Now, however, the tables were turned. Lazarus was being comforted, and the rich man was being tormented.

It might seem that the rich man had had a change of heart, but alas, it was probably not the case. As someone said, "True repentance is seldom late, and late repentance is seldom true!" So we might well question whether the rich man had really changed. He was still centered on his own needs and still trying to order people around! Even if Abraham had wanted to grant the request of the rich man, he cited a simple reason why he could not: "Between us and you there is a great gulf fixed" (vs. 26). There will be no travel between heaven and hell. One's eternal destiny is fixed at death. While some suggest that God might give people a second chance after death, there is no hint of this in the Bible. As was true for the rich man, if we go to hell, it will be too late to do anything about it!

Great tragedy (Luke 16:27-28). Since Lazarus could not leave paradise to aid him in his torment, the rich man made another request. He pleaded that Lazarus might be sent back to earth for the purpose of warning the rich man's unrepentant brothers. While nothing else is said about these brothers, they too must have pursued selfish, ungodly lives.

REVELATION SUFFICIENT—
Luke 16:29-31

Hear God's Word (Luke 16:29-30). What might sound like an appropriate request to prevent others from being eternally lost was answered very succinctly by Abraham: "They have Moses and the prophets." In short, what revelation they already had from God was sufficient. The testimony of God's Word, whether the Old Testament for those who were under the old covenant or the completed Bible for people today, is all that is needed. We only need to listen to Scripture and believe what God says (Rom. 10:17)!

The rich man persisted, however. He argued that a miraculous demonstration—Lazarus returning from the dead—would convince his brothers and cause them to repent.

Heed God's Word (Luke 16:31). Abraham replied that if the brothers would not heed the Scriptures, they would not be persuaded by a man who returned from the dead. Indeed, even Jesus' miracles did not convince His opponents that He was the Messiah.

"Jesus was obviously suggesting that the rich man symbolized the Pharisees. They wanted signs—signs so clear that they would compel people to believe. But since they refused to believe the Scriptures, they would not believe any sign no matter how great. Just a short time later Jesus did raise a man from the dead, another man named Lazarus (John 11:38-44). The result was that the religious leaders began to plot more earnestly to kill both Jesus and Lazarus (John 11:45-53; 12:10-11)" (Walvoord and Zuck).

—*John Alva Owston.*

QUESTIONS

1. What is the traditional name given the rich man? Where does it come from?
2. How is the rich man's lifestyle described?
3. Who was Lazarus, and how is he described?
4. What happened to both men once they died?
5. What is the word translated "hell" in this passage, and to what does it refer?
6. What did the rich man want Lazarus to do for him?
7. Why was it not possible for Abraham to fulfill the rich man's request?
8. What additional request did the rich man have?
9. What information did the rich man and his brothers already have?
10. How does this story relate to the Pharisees and their rejection of Christ?

—*John Alva Owston.*

PRACTICAL POINTS

1. When we have the opportunity, we should help those who are in need (Luke 16:19-21; cf. Gal. 6:10).
2. One who refuses to show kindness in this life should not expect any in the next (Luke 16:22-24).
3. One day, all people will be held accountable for their actions (vss. 25-26).
4. We should tell our loved ones about Jesus while we still can (vss. 27-28).
5. The Word of God contains everything we need to know about salvation (vss. 29-30).
6. If a person's heart is closed off to God, the greatest miracle will have no effect on him (vs. 31).

—*Charity G. Carter.*

RESEARCH AND DISCUSSION

1. Why did the rich man ignore Lazarus every day (Luke 16:19-20)?
2. Explain the irony of the rich man asking Abraham to send Lazarus to place a drop of water on his tongue (vs. 24).
3. What does verse 25 mean? Will some people who have more than enough on earth not be able to enter heaven?
4. What spiritual gulf in this life separates people who do not know God from those who do (vs. 26)? What can the people of God do to bridge that gap?
5. Why did the rich man believe that his brothers would listen to Lazarus when they had not listened to anyone else (vss. 27-29)?

—*Charity G. Carter.*

Golden Text Illuminated

"Son, remember that thou in thy lifetime receivedst thy good things, and likewise Lazarus evil things: but now he is comforted, and thou art tormented" (Luke 16:25).

The rich man and Lazarus had contrasting lives and destinies, and their story has a striking twist. The rich man had all the "good" things in life, which we see from Luke 16:19 included a prosperous lifestyle, with nice clothes and whatever he wanted to eat.

On the other hand, Lazarus was a beggar who lay out in the street. He was physically unwell and did not get enough to eat. This is the classic contrast between the haves and the have nots. Some experience great prosperity, and some suffer great loss.

The interesting thing is that the Lord went on to show that how one fares materially in this life does not determine one's destiny in the next. The rich man and Lazarus had contrasting destinies, and they were not what the world would expect. Lazarus's deprived earthly condition did not prevent him from entering paradise. He was, in fact, saved and ushered to "Abraham's bosom" (vs. 22) by the angels of God.

The rich man, on the other hand, was not saved. It was a shock for him to find himself in torment after death. He learned that this end was fixed and nonnegotiable as he sought to bargain with Abraham (vss. 23-26).

So we see great contrasts in the Lord's story of Lazarus and the rich man. The message is stark and plain. Help us, Lord, to preach this plain message for all to hear!

—*Jeff VanGoethem.*

LESSON 8   JULY 23, 2023

Scripture Lesson Text

MATT. 25:31 When the Son of man shall come in his glory, and all the holy angels with him, then shall he sit upon the throne of his glory:

32 And before him shall be gathered all nations: and he shall separate them one from another, as a shepherd divideth *his* **sheep from the goats:**

33 And he shall set the sheep on his right hand, but the goats on the left.

34 Then shall the King say unto them on his right hand, Come, ye blessed of my Father, inherit the kingdom prepared for you from the foundation of the world:

35 For I was an hungred, and ye gave me meat: I was thirsty, and ye gave me drink: I was a stranger, and ye took me in:

36 Naked, and ye clothed me: I was sick, and ye visited me: I was in prison, and ye came unto me.

37 Then shall the righteous answer him, saying, Lord, when saw we thee an hungred, and fed *thee*? or thirsty, and gave *thee* drink?

38 When saw we thee a stranger, and took *thee* **in? or naked, and clothed** *thee***?**

39 Or when saw we thee sick, or in prison, and came unto thee?

40 And the King shall answer and say unto them, Verily I say unto you, Inasmuch as ye have done *it* **unto one of the least of these my brethren, ye have done** *it* **unto me.**

41 Then shall he say also unto them on the left hand, Depart from me, ye cursed, into everlasting fire, prepared for the devil and his angels:

42 For I was an hungred, and ye gave me no meat: I was thirsty, and ye gave me no drink:

43 I was a stranger, and ye took me not in: naked, and ye clothed me not: sick, and in prison, and ye visited me not.

44 Then shall they also answer him, saying, Lord, when saw we thee an hungred, or athirst, or a stranger, or naked, or sick, or in prison, and did not minister unto thee?

45 Then shall he answer them, saying, Verily I say unto you, Inasmuch as ye did *it* not to one of the least of these, ye did *it* not to me.

46 And these shall go away into everlasting punishment: but the righteous into life eternal.

NOTES

Separating the Sheep and the Goats

Lesson Text: Matthew 25:31-46

Related Scriptures: Deuteronomy 15:7-11; Daniel 7:9-14; Matthew 16:24-28; I John 4:7-14

TIME: A.D. 30   PLACE: Jerusalem

GOLDEN TEXT—"And these shall go away into everlasting punishment: but the righteous into life eternal" (Matthew 25:46).

Lesson Exposition

Among the works that reveal the true heart of a believer is that of helping to meet the needs of others. This is so important that in the final judgment of the nations, Christ will point to what they did or did not do for others.

JUDGING THE RIGHTEOUS—Matt. 25:31-36

A gathering (Matt. 25:31-32). The text of this week's study reveals the importance of present living in the light of future events more clearly than any other passage in Matthew. What Jesus referred to in these verses is the last eschatological, or end-time, event prior to the establishment of the millennial kingdom.

The Son of man will come and be given a throne of glory. All the nations will come before Him, and He will separate believers from unbelievers.

A dividing (Matt. 25:33-34). Jesus referred to those on His right hand as sheep and to those on His left as goats. The sheep represent believers, while the goats represent unbelievers.

It is the group on Christ's right hand that will be invited to enter into the kingdom with Him. Throughout the Bible the place at the right hand is viewed as the place of honor and authority (Pss. 45:9; 110:1).

A pronouncement (Matt. 25:35-36). At this point Jesus explains why this group is being invited to enter the kingdom. When He was hungry, they gave Him food. When He was thirsty, they gave Him drink. When He was a stranger, they took Him in and cared for Him. When He was naked, they gave Him clothing. When He was sick, they visited Him and nursed Him. When He was in prison, they came to Him, revealing their caring hearts.

These are six needy conditions that represent the kinds of needs all people experience at one time or another. Jesus speaks as if these actions were done directly for Him, meeting needs He faced personally.

EVIDENCES OF RIGHTEOUSNESS—Matt. 25:37-40

A sense of confusion (Matt. 25:37-39). The group at the right hand of Jesus, previously called sheep, is now referred to as "the righteous." They are portrayed as being confused and surprised at the descriptions they had just heard. They do not remember even seeing Him, let alone doing these things for His personal benefit.

As we anticipate Christ's coming, we must remain aware of the needs people face daily.

A reassurance (Matt. 25:40). The phrase "unto one of the least of these my brethren" has been understood in several different ways. Since those gathered are divided into two categories designated as sheep and goats, these "brethren" appear to be another, separate group. Of course, it is possible Jesus was simply referring to those who had needs to whom others reached out, ministering unselfishly. The point is obvious: we are not saved just to care for ourselves; we are saved to be concerned and to reach out to meet the needs that fellow believers us are facing.

JUDGING THE UNRIGHTEOUS—Matt. 25:41-46

Damnation (Matt. 25:41). Jesus then explains what will happen to those at His left side. They will be commanded to depart, being referred to as "ye cursed." Their destination is "everlasting fire," a description of hell, which has been prepared for Satan and his angels. No pretender will ever be able to deceive the Lord.

Condemnation (Matt. 25:42-43). The King now lists the same six physical needs He mentioned to the righteous. This time, however, He declares that this group did not meet any of those needs. They are totally self-centered.

Affirmation (Matt. 25:44-45). The people in this group also seem confused and surprised. They have not seen Jesus either and wonder when they could possibly have missed doing these things. Jesus explains that when they refused to reach out and help "one of the least of these," they in essence refused to help Him.

Separation (Matt. 25:46). There are two categories of people. People are either believers in Christ or unbelievers who refuse to trust in Him. There are also two destinies, heaven and hell. Heaven is where God dwells and where believers will live for all eternity. It is described in the Bible as a beautiful place of joy, peace, and contentment. Hell is described as a place of eternal torment.

—*Keith E. Eggert.*

QUESTIONS

1. When will the event that Jesus speaks of in Matthew 25:31 take place?
2. How did Jesus refer to the two groups of people?
3. Which group will be invited to enter the kingdom?
4. What is the significance of the right-hand side in Scripture?
5. What does Jesus say they did to qualify them for this particular invitation?
6. Why are they surprised and confused by Jesus' statement?
7. What practical lesson should we learn from this?
8. What is Jesus' message for the ones at His left side?
9. How does Jesus explain this decision?
10. What are the two eternal destinies, and what determines one's destiny?

—*Keith E. Eggert.*

PRACTICAL POINTS

1. We need to be conscious of the fact that everyone we know and meet will one day stand before the Lord (Matt. 25:31-33).
2. It is comforting to know that we have been in God's plan from the beginning (vs. 34).
3. The best way to serve the Lord is to meet the real needs of other people (vss. 35-40).
4. The fate of all who reject Christ should motivate us to proclaim the gospel (vs. 41).
5. A lack of compassion for hurting people shows a lack of love for the Lord (vss. 42-45).
6. How we live today reveals where we will be in eternity (vs. 46).

—Jarl K. Waggoner.

RESEARCH AND DISCUSSION

1. How does the description in Matthew 25:31-46 differ from the one given in Revelation 20:11-15?
2. Why is the compassionate treatment of other people, rather than what one believes, set forth as the measure of one's salvation (Matt. 25:34-38)?
3. What role should the church have in helping the poor and hurting? Would it be proper to seek government assistance in doing so?
4. Does the reaction of both the "sheep" (vss. 37-39) and the "goats" (vs. 44) suggest that a person can never know for sure in this life whether he is truly saved? Explain.
5. What principles for ministry does Jesus' parable give us?

—Jarl K. Waggoner.

Golden Text Illuminated

"And these shall go away into everlasting punishment: but the righteous into life eternal" (Matthew 25:46).

The concluding words of what is called Jesus' Olivet Discourse make very clear that there are only two possible eternal destinations for mankind. People will either suffer "everlasting punishment," or they will enjoy joyous eternal life.

Needless to say, this stark reality is not popular in the unsaved world. Yet when we recognize man's fallen condition, it becomes a matter of sheer grace on God's part that He provided a way of deliverance and renewed fellowship with Him through Christ. As has often been said, the real wonder is that God chose to save anyone at all in the face of man's continual rebellion.

Equally important, God is the Creator. He breathes life into every creature on the earth, including man. He is the very source of life. When man rejects God, he is rejecting life itself.

So those whose lives demonstrate that they have rejected the eternal Son of God will experience everlasting punishment (cf. Dan. 12:2), and many Scriptures give vivid pictures of the severity of that judgment. It is *eternal* punishment—of the same duration that is described for the enjoyment of the blessed.

The best way to answer skeptics is to give them glimpses of what eternal life is like by the joy and love evident in our lives. Eternal life does mean living forever in heaven, but the term also involves a quality of life, a reflection of what it means to live in fellowship with the eternally good and perfect God.

—Stephen H. Barnhart.

LESSON 9   **JULY 30, 2023**

Scripture Lesson Text

MATT. 13:9 Who hath ears to hear, let him hear.

10 And the disciples came, and said unto him, Why speakest thou unto them in parables?

11 He answered and said unto them, Because it is given unto you to know the mysteries of the kingdom of heaven, but to them it is not given.

12 For whosoever hath, to him shall be given, and he shall have more abundance: but whosoever hath not, from him shall be taken away even that he hath.

13 Therefore speak I to them in parables: because they seeing see not; and hearing they hear not, neither do they understand.

14 And in them is fulfilled the prophecy of Esaias, which saith, By hearing ye shall hear, and shall not understand; and seeing ye shall see, and shall not perceive:

15 For this people's heart is waxed gross, and *their* ears are dull of hearing, and their eyes they have closed; lest at any time they should see with *their* eyes, and hear with *their* ears, and should understand with *their* heart, and should be converted, and I should heal them.

16 But blessed *are* your eyes, for they see: and your ears, for they hear.

17 For verily I say unto you, That many prophets and righteous *men* have desired to see *those things* which ye see, and have not seen *them;* and to hear *those things* which ye hear, and have not heard *them.*

NOTES

Ears to Hear

Lesson Text: Matthew 13:9-17

Related Scriptures: Matthew 13:18-23; I Corinthians 2:6-16

TIME: A.D. 28   PLACE: Sea of Galilee

GOLDEN TEXT—"Who hath ears to hear, let him hear" (Matthew 13:9).

Lesson Exposition

THE IMPORTANCE OF LISTENING—Matt. 13:9-13

Hearing parables (Matt. 13:9-10). In New Testament days, there were ungodly people who apparently had a curious interest in spiritual matters but were not interested in embracing the gospel of Jesus Christ. From them spiritual truth was withheld. When Jesus taught His disciples, He used a method of teaching that kept ungodly listeners from comprehending what He was saying. When He said, "Who hath ears to hear, let him hear" (vs. 9), He was referring to the godly.

Jesus had just finished telling the parable of the sower (vss. 3-8). As we find out later in the chapter, even the disciples could not initially understand the meaning of this parable (vss. 18-23). But when it was explained to them, they would have the capability of comprehending the message Jesus conveyed. They were puzzled, however, as to why Jesus was teaching in parables.

Hearing and understanding (Matt. 13:11-12a). Jesus had offered Himself to Israel as her Messiah, but she had rejected Him. The epitome of the rejection can be seen in the statement in Matthew 12:24. The religious leaders had concluded, "This fellow doth not cast out devils, but by Beelzebub the prince of the devils." In saying this they attributed His power and authority to Satan. It appears that it was after this rejection that Jesus began teaching in parables much more extensively. The disciples noticed the different emphasis and asked Jesus the reason for it.

In response to their question about teaching in parables, Jesus gave three reasons. The first is given in these verses. Jesus wanted to pass on to His followers the mysteries of the kingdom of heaven.

Those who believed in the Lord were enjoying the privilege of learning more about Him, His Father, and the eternal plan coming from them. Those who rejected the Lord were being denied any further comprehension because of their refusal to believe. This still occurs today. Those who receive the Saviour are given insight into the Word of God, while those who reject Him cannot understand it.

Hearing and not understanding (Matt. 13:12b-13). The second reason Jesus gave for teaching in parables was His desire to hide spiritual insight from those who were rejecting Him. We saw this fact as part of His first reason, but He especially emphasized it in these verses. Verse 11 includes the phrase "to them it is not given," indicating that those outside the circle of believers were not being given the same spiritual instruction as the believers. Not understanding the truth, they soon forget it. It is snatched away from their hearts by the enemy.

Jesus described such a person as one who saw but did not see and heard but did not hear. Those who rejected Him saw Him teaching the people and listened to His words, but they could not understand His messages. They had physical hearing without an ability to hear spiritually. They had physical sight without an ability to comprehend spiritual reality.

THE DISCREPANCIES IN LISTENING—Matt. 13:14-17

Isaiah's prophecy (Matt. 13:14-15). These words are quoted from Isaiah 6:9-10. Isaiah 6 records the call of Isaiah to his prophetic ministry.

Isaiah was to tell the people to keep listening without understanding and to keep looking without perceiving. By Isaiah's time, Israel was so corrupt that God would not turn from His determination to punish her with captivity. Sadly, Judah, the southern kingdom, was also filled with corruption.

Since the hearts of the people in Isaiah's day were already hardened against God, the more he preached, the more hardened they would become. As he ministered, their hearts would become increasingly dull, their ears would become less receptive to this message, and their eyes would remain blinded to the truth. They had reached the point in their rejection of God where He refused to enable them to turn back and be healed.

The same thing that happened to the people in Isaiah's day was now happening in Jesus' day. People had rejected God and the Messiah He had sent. To fulfill Isaiah's prophecy was the third reason Jesus spoke in parables. Just as in Isaiah's time, there would be a remnant of believers, but on the whole, the people were rejecting Him and would suffer the consequences.

The disciples' blessing (Matt. 13:16-17). The disciples were a great contrast to those who rejected Jesus, and as a result they were unusually blessed. They had believed that Jesus was indeed the Messiah sent from God; therefore, they were able to comprehend further spiritual truths. That is completely the opposite of those who had no spiritual comprehension at all. This contrast still applies between believers and nonbelievers.

—Keith E. Eggert.

QUESTIONS

1. What type of people among those listening to Jesus could not comprehend what He was saying?
2. What question did the disciples ask Jesus, and why?
3. At what point in His ministry did Jesus begin to use parables more extensively?
4. What were the first two reasons Jesus gave for using parables?
5. What does the phrase "to them it is not given" mean (Matt. 13:11)?
6. What happens in the hearts of people today when they reject the truth after they hear it?
7. How can people see but not see?
8. Who did Jesus quote, and what was the context of that quote?
9. How did that Old Testament passage apply in Jesus' day?
10. How were the disciples blessed in an unusually wonderful way?

—Keith E. Eggert.

Adult Bible Class

PRACTICAL POINTS

1. We should take advantage of every opportunity to hear God's Word (Matt. 13:9).
2. We cannot know God's plans apart from His gracious revelation of them (vss. 10-11).
3. Spiritual truth can be grasped only by those who are indwelt by God's Spirit (vss. 12-13).
4. Hearing God's truth is of no value unless the hearing is accompanied by faith (vss. 14-15).
5. We should never take for granted the divine blessing of spiritual understanding (vs. 16).
6. The privilege of having God's full revelation obligates us to learn it and live it (vs. 17).

—Jarl K. Waggoner.

RESEARCH AND DISCUSSION

1. Is there ever any reason for us to withhold God's truth from particular individuals (Matt. 13:10-11)? Why or why not?
2. What is required for us to fully understand God's revelation (vss. 12-13)?
3. Have you encountered people who have heard God's Word repeatedly but never understood it (vss. 14-15)? What accounts for this? Is it fruitless to try to reach them with the gospel? Why or why not?
4. What are some of the blessings we enjoy that the Old Testament saints did not (vss. 16-17)?
5. What does Jesus' teaching in parables tell us about the character of God and how He deals with mankind?

—Jarl K. Waggoner.

Golden Text Illuminated

"Who hath ears to hear, let him hear" (Matthew 13:9).

Our golden text appears at the end of a parable. The word "parable" refers to something set alongside; thus, it is a story set alongside some spiritual truth and meant to illustrate it. A parable was a story that might need interpretation, and those who wanted to learn the meaning of it would ask (cf. Matt. 13:36). Jesus was a master of every teaching method He used, and this was true of His use of parables. He used them to separate the spiritually hungry from those with no interest at all.

Our golden text was in itself a miniparable. Everyone has physical ears. Obviously, some with ears may in fact be deaf, but the point Jesus was making was that some people also have spiritual ears. The person who had an interest in spiritual matters would either understand the intent of the story or would seek it by asking that it be explained to him. Those who had no interest in learning spiritual truths would go on their way, content to have heard a nice little story.

Those with spiritual ears are those intent on hearing anew what the Holy Spirit will say to them. These same people are usually the ones who ask for clarification if they do not understand the point being made.

We also must personally apply the challenge of the golden text to ourselves. Do we come to Bible studies or church services with ears to hear, or do we inwardly tune out familiar texts? "Who hath ears to hear, let him hear" is spoken to us as much as it is to our neighbors in the pew.

—Darrell W. McKay.

LESSON 10   AUGUST 6, 2023

Scripture Lesson Text

MATT. 18:21 Then came Peter to him, and said, Lord, how oft shall my brother sin against me, and I forgive him? till seven times?

22 Jesus saith unto him, I say not unto thee, Until seven times: but, Until seventy times seven.

23 Therefore is the kingdom of heaven likened unto a certain king, which would take account of his servants.

24 And when he had begun to reckon, one was brought unto him, which owed him ten thousand talents.

25 But forasmuch as he had not to pay, his lord commanded him to be sold, and his wife, and children, and all that he had, and payment to be made.

26 The servant therefore fell down, and worshipped him, saying, Lord, have patience with me, and I will pay thee all.

27 Then the lord of that servant was moved with compassion, and loosed him, and forgave him the debt.

28 But the same servant went out, and found one of his fellowservants, which owed him an hundred pence: and he laid hands on him, and took *him* by the throat, saying, Pay me that thou owest.

29 And his fellowservant fell down at his feet, and besought him, saying, Have patience with me, and I will pay thee all.

30 And he would not: but went and cast him into prison, till he should pay the debt.

31 So when his fellowservants saw what was done, they were very sorry, and came and told unto their lord all that was done.

32 Then his lord, after that he had called him, said unto him, O thou wicked servant, I forgave thee all that debt, because thou desiredst me:

33 Shouldest not thou also have had compassion on thy fellowservant, even as I had pity on thee?

34 And his lord was wroth, and delivered him to the tormentors, till he should pay all that was due unto him.

35 So likewise shall my heavenly Father do also unto you, if ye from your hearts forgive not every one his brother their trespasses.

NOTES

Adult Bible Class   47

Forgiving One Another

Lesson Text: Matthew 18:21-35

Related Scriptures: Luke 6:27-38; 17:1-4

TIME: A.D. 29   PLACE: Capernaum

GOLDEN TEXT—"Then his lord, after that he had called him, said unto him, O thou wicked servant, I forgave thee all that debt, because thou desiredst me: shouldest not thou also have had compassion on thy fellowservant, even as I had pity on thee?" (Matthew 18:32-33).

Lesson Exposition

THE SERVANT FORGIVEN—Matt. 18:21-27

Seeking guidance (Matt. 18:21-22). Jesus had just finished telling the disciples how believers are to handle someone who has sinned against them. Peter had a logical follow-up question: How often are we required to forgive a person who repeatedly sins against us? In suggesting seven times, Peter was actually being generous, for the rabbis taught that a person should forgive someone who has sinned against him up to three times.

It is important to note that Peter was asking about a relationship between believers. This is evident from the term "my brother" (vs. 21).

Jesus' answer did not mean we should count up to 490 offenses! He was teaching that forgiveness should go on endlessly, no matter how many times we are offended. A child of God should never carry a grudge.

Settling accounts (Matt. 18:23-24). Jesus then told of a king who wanted to settle accounts with his servants. The man brought before him owed ten thousand talents, which in our economy would amount to millions of dollars.

This man found himself in a hopeless position. He faced a debt he had no way to pay, and yet his master was demanding to have the account settled right then. The concept of debt can be applied to offenses because when we find ourselves offended by someone, we feel the person owes us something to make up for it.

Releasing debts (Matt. 18:25-27). When it was realized that the king's servant would not be able to pay his debt, the king ordered that he, his wife, his children, and all his property be sold and the money used to settle part of the debt. The servant fell down before his master, begging for an extension of time and promising to pay it all off—a totally unrealistic request.

In the most amazing move he could possibly make, the king forgave his servant the entire debt and released him from the obligation of paying any of it back. No doubt Jesus purposely used such a huge amount of debt in His parable to clearly demonstrate the greatness of God's forgiveness of our sins.

THE SERVANT UNFORGIVING—
Matt. 18:28-35

Demanding payment (Matt. 18:28-29). The situation here is similar to the previous one in that it involves a creditor and a debtor; however, the man who had been forgiven his debt by the king responded very differently to a man who owed him money. One of his fellow servants owed him one hundred denarii. This would amount to a little over three months' wages, which was no small sum. It was minuscule, however, compared to what he had been forgiven.

The first servant treated his fellow servant roughly and thoughtlessly. He took him by the throat, apparently choking him, and demanding payment of what was owed him. Just as this man had done before the king, his fellow servant fell down before him, pleading for time and promising to repay everything. Everything the first servant did indicated a completely merciless attitude.

We must keep in mind that this is a parable, not an actual incident. The Lord purposely set up an immense contrast in order to make His point. We must also keep in mind that in a parable, not every detail demands an application.

Reporting injustice (Matt. 18:30-31). The merciless attitude of the first servant caused him to ignore the pleading of his fellow servant. He had him thrown into prison until he could repay everything. His action infuriated and grieved the other servants. They went to the master and reported everything that had happened.

Confronting inequity (Matt. 18:32-33). Once again the first servant was called into the presence of his master, the king, who was very angry about what he had heard.

The master confronted his servant. He asked this pointed question: "Shouldest not thou also have had compassion on thy fellowservant, even as I had pity on thee?" (vs. 33). It is clear that Jesus expects His followers, who have been forgiven, to be forgiving.

Teaching forgiveness (Matt. 18:34-35). The master immediately had the first servant thrown into prison. Jesus summarized by saying, "So likewise shall my heavenly Father do also unto you, if ye from your hearts forgive not every one his brother their trespasses." Jesus' words teach us a lot about how the lives of His people are to be transformed. A forgiving spirit does not earn salvation, but it certainly is an evidence of a regenerated heart.

This would be a good time for each of us to examine our heart and be certain that there is no spirit of bitterness or unwillingness to forgive.

—Keith E. Eggert.

QUESTIONS

1. What had caused Peter to wonder about how often to forgive?
2. How do we know his concern was about fellow believers?
3. How did Jesus respond to Peter's seemingly generous offer to forgive seven times? What did He mean?
4. How does the concept of debt relate to our need to forgive?
5. What was Jesus portraying in the first servant's huge debt?
6. What did the servant do after being forgiven, and what did this reveal about him?
7. What must we keep in mind about interpreting a parable?
8. How did the master respond to what he heard about the servant?
9. What does this parable teach?
10. What is a practical way in which we can apply this parable?

—Keith E. Eggert.

PRACTICAL POINTS

1. Followers of Christ do not have the option of withholding forgiveness (Matt. 18:21-22).
2. Forgiveness is not something that is earned; it is something that is given (vss. 23-27).
3. If we do not forgive, we demonstrate ingratitude for God's forgiveness of us (vss. 28-30).
4. Hypocrisy and a lack of mercy are sins that cannot be hidden (vss. 31-33).
5. An unforgiving spirit brings God's displeasure, as well as His discipline (vs. 34).
6. Forgiveness that is not heartfelt is no forgiveness at all (vs. 35).

—Jarl K. Waggoner.

RESEARCH AND DISCUSSION

1. What attitude do you think prompted Peter's question (Matt. 18:21)? What did he not understand about forgiveness?
2. Are there no limits at all on forgiveness (vs. 22)? Do we do others harm by routinely forgiving them for repeated offenses?
3. Why do you think Jesus used a story to illustrate the answer He had given Peter (vss. 23-34)?
4. What does an unwillingness to forgive others reveal about us?
5. Should we forgive even those who do not ask for forgiveness?
6. How can we be sure that we are truly forgiving others from the heart and not simply going through the motions (vs. 35)?

—Jarl K. Waggoner.

Golden Text Illuminated

"Then his lord, after that he had called him, said unto him, O thou wicked servant, I forgave thee all that debt, because thou desiredst me: shouldest not thou also have had compassion on thy fellowservant, even as I had pity on thee?" (Matthew 18:32-33).

Our world is full of fractured relationships. In the Parable of the Unmerciful Servant, Jesus masterfully illustrates one reason for that. Sinful man desperately needs and seeks mercy for himself, but he has the tendency to demand strict justice for everyone else, particularly when it comes to what he believes is his due.

This week's golden text expresses the moral of Jesus' parable as the king exposes the hypocrisy of his wicked servant. He had been forgiven so much ("all that debt"), but then he showed no patience with a man who owed him much less.

In this case, mercy over a financial matter is the example used. But the truth urged here also applies to all areas that call for mercy or forgiveness.

In the Lord's Prayer, which is to serve as a model for our interaction with God, we are told to ask the Lord to "forgive us our debts, as we forgive our debtors" (Matt. 6:12).

Does this mean that we have to earn our salvation by doing certain things? No, what it means is that our actions reveal whether we have a genuine relationship with God. If we are unwilling to extend mercy to others, do we really have a heart knowledge of God's character that is born out of a genuine relationship with Him?

—Stephen H. Barnhart.

LESSON 11   **AUGUST 13, 2023**

Scripture Lesson Text

LUKE 15:11 And he said, A certain man had two sons:

12 And the younger of them said to *his* father, Father, give me the portion of goods that falleth *to me.* And he divided unto them *his* living.

13 And not many days after the younger son gathered all together, and took his journey into a far country, and there wasted his substance with riotous living.

14 And when he had spent all, there arose a mighty famine in that land; and he began to be in want.

15 And he went and joined himself to a citizen of that country; and he sent him into his fields to feed swine.

16 And he would fain have filled his belly with the husks that the swine did eat: and no man gave unto him.

17 And when he came to himself, he said, How many hired servants of my father's have bread enough and to spare, and I perish with hunger!

18 I will arise and go to my father, and will say unto him, Father, I have sinned against heaven, and before thee,

19 And am no more worthy to be called thy son: make me as one of thy hired servants.

20 And he arose, and came to his father. But when he was yet a great way off, his father saw him, and had compassion, and ran, and fell on his neck, and kissed him.

21 And the son said unto him, Father, I have sinned against heaven, and in thy sight, and am no more worthy to be called thy son.

22 But the father said to his servants, Bring forth the best robe, and put *it* on him; and put a ring on his hand, and shoes on *his* feet:

23 And bring hither the fatted calf, and kill *it;* and let us eat, and be merry:

24 For this my son was dead, and is alive again; he was lost, and is found. And they began to be merry.

NOTES

A Story of Forgiveness

Lesson Text: Luke 15:11-24

Related Scriptures: Luke 15:25-32; Romans 12:9-21; II Corinthians 5:17-21

TIME: A.D. 30   PLACE: probably Perea

GOLDEN TEXT—"This my son was dead, and is alive again; he was lost, and is found" (Luke 15:24).

Lesson Exposition

A BROKEN RELATIONSHIP—Luke 15:11-16

The son's request (Luke 15:11-12). This is the third of three connected parables. It is about a man and his two sons. For some unknown reason, the younger son asked for his portion of the inheritance early.

The father's response was a very gracious and generous act on his part. He did not force his son to stay with him but instead granted his request by giving him his portion of the inheritance early.

In order to understand the parable, we need to recognize that the father represents God, the older brother represents the religious leaders, and the younger brother represents sinners.

The son's wastefulness (Luke 15:13-14). As planned, the younger son took his new fortune and left home, traveling to another country a good distance away. He must have become something of a party animal, making himself popular with everybody because of his willingness to spend money on them. The Greek word translated "wasted" means "to dissipate" or "to squander."

The son's desperation (Luke 15:15-16). When things turned desperate, he hired himself out to a Gentile pig farmer, caring for animals that were unclean to Jews. As evidence of his destitution, he became so hungry that he wanted to eat their food.

To feed pigs was great humiliation for a Jewish young man, and to eat their food was complete degradation.

A RESTORED RELATIONSHIP—Luke 15:17-24

The son's decision (Luke 15:17-19). It was while sitting among the pigs that were better fed than he was that he finally came to his senses and thought about home. He realized that what he had run from was far better than anything he had found since. This is a good testimony to the quality of homelife he had once enjoyed. How many parents wait and long for their child to come to a realization like this? Jesus' story can be a means of encouragement and hope for such parents.

If his father would allow it, he would return to his home, confess his sin, and ask to be allowed to live there as a servant. That way he could at least have food regularly. He had reached the point where all he could hope for was mercy. Note that he planned to admit his sin not only against his father, but also against God.

The son's return (Luke 15:20-21). "Finally, his mind went to work again. Humans have the capacity to change. We do not have to remain in the pigpen. We do not have to continue to live as sinners. We can become responsible for our lives. We can quit our riotous living. We can come home" (Anders, ed., *Holman New Testament Commentary,* Broadman & Holman). When the young man returned, the father's response was priceless! He had been watching every day for his son. When he saw him, his fatherly compassion rose to the fore, and he ran to meet him.

The son was still a long way off when his father spotted him. His longing for his son's return is fully evident in his actions. Imagine if he had not been watching in this manner and if the son had arrived at his door before he knew he was anywhere around. We cannot help noticing that the focus of attention has now changed from the son to the father. Jesus made this shift on purpose in order to portray His Father as the loving God waiting for the return of those He loves so dearly.

The father's welcome (Luke 15:22-24). Contrary to the son's intent to be a hired servant, the father made him a full member of the family again. He gave him a standing like that which he had previously, one that was full of privileges. He had the best robe brought out and put on him, along with a ring, and sandals for his feet. Since hired servants probably went barefoot, this was a clear indication that the father was receiving him back as his son and not as a hired servant.

The fatted calf was reserved for a banquet of celebration, usually during one of the national feasts. The boy's return was cause enough for the father to celebrate. Did you notice that he was so eager for his son's return that he ran to meet him (vs. 20), something that no dignified man in that culture would do? Since this father's joy is a reflection of God's when someone comes back to Him, we need to reflect on these moments.

This father portrays our Heavenly Father in His love, kindness, grace, and mercy. If any one of us needs to be reconciled to Him, we can be certain that He is waiting and watching and will never turn away someone coming to Him. For this young man, the return was just the beginning. From then on, his relationship with his father would no doubt be full of blessings.

—Keith E. Eggert.

QUESTIONS

1. How did the father respond to his son's arrogant request?
2. What persons or groups are portrayed by the parable?
3. What did the son do after receiving what he asked for?
4. What was especially degrading about the son's circumstances and employment?
5. What brought him to his senses, and what did he decide to do?
6. How do we know the father never stopped longing for his son?
7. Why did Jesus shift the attention of His parable from the son to the father?
8. What did the father do to restore and rejoice over his son?
9. Why is it important that we focus on the father?
10. What does this reconciliation show us about God our Father?

—Keith E. Eggert.

PRACTICAL POINTS

1. Affluence absent spiritual discernment often leads to a squandering of it all (Luke 15:11-13).
2. The world is a cruel place to those who have foolishly lost everything (vss. 14-16).
3. Sometimes we have to hit bottom before we wise up (vs. 17).
4. We try to bargain with God; He wants to show us His grace (vss. 18-20).
5. We really are not worthy to be called God's children; thankfully, it does not depend on that (vss. 21-22).
6. We should join heaven in celebrating every time a lost sinner is found (vss. 23-24).

—Kenneth A. Sponsler.

RESEARCH AND DISCUSSION

1. Why did the father agree to such an offensive and unprecedented request (Luke 15:12)? What does this tell us about God and His dealings with us?
2. Why is the allure of a far country and wild living so strong for many young people (vs. 13)? Could the father have done anything to allay it?
3. Everyone suffers in a famine. Why was it especially hard on the wayward son (vss. 14-16)?
4. Do you think the son was sincere in his plan to confess sinning against his father and heaven (vss. 18-19)? Why or why not?
5. Why was such an extravagant celebration appropriate for the wayward son's empty-handed return after wasting his father's money (vss. 22-24)? How does this apply to us?

—Kenneth A. Sponsler.

Golden Text Illuminated

"This my son was dead, and is alive again; he was lost, and is found" (Luke 15:24).

In 1961, the world was stunned when the Berlin Wall was erected. After World War II, Germany had been split into four sections, each controlled by a different country. While the West offered freedom, the Soviet Union tightened its grip. Germany was divided into East and West.

In the same way, sin creates a barrier between God and us. When sin initially creeps into our lives, we may not think much about it. Often we rationalize it: "It is only just this one time." That sin seems small and insignificant.

However, sin grows swiftly. Just as the Berlin Wall was erected section by section, so a wall is built up in our souls. In a short time, we discover that our prayer lives are lacking and our walk has grown stale. We are trapped by the barrier.

As the families separated by the Berlin Wall longed to be reunited, so our Father yearns for us. When the sin wall went up, His family was torn apart. We are the relatives on the other side whom He misses.

However, His righteousness is such that there can be no sin in His presence. Thus, we are unable to break down the sin wall by our own volition.

When we turn to God and become reconciled to Him, there is nothing that can separate us from His love through Christ (Rom. 8:38-39). His Word tells us that there is great joy in being reconciled to God (5:10-11). Even the angels rejoice (Luke 15:7).

—Jennifer Lautermilch.

LESSON 12 **AUGUST 20, 2023**

Scripture Lesson Text

MATT. 20:1 For the kingdom of heaven is like unto a man *that is* an householder, which went out early in the morning to hire labourers into his vineyard.

2 And when he had agreed with the labourers for a penny a day, he sent them into his vineyard.

3 And he went out about the third hour, and saw others standing idle in the marketplace,

4 And said unto them; Go ye also into the vineyard, and whatsoever is right I will give you. And they went their way.

5 Again he went out about the sixth and ninth hour, and did likewise.

6 And about the eleventh hour he went out, and found others standing idle, and saith unto them, Why stand ye here all the day idle?

7 They say unto him, Because no man hath hired us. He saith unto them, Go ye also into the vineyard; and whatsoever is right, *that* shall ye receive.

8 So when even was come, the lord of the vineyard saith unto his steward, Call the labourers, and give them *their* hire, beginning from the last unto the first.

9 And when they came that *were hired* about the eleventh hour, they received every man a penny.

10 But when the first came, they supposed that they should have received more; and they likewise received every man a penny.

11 And when they had received *it,* they murmured against the goodman of the house,

12 Saying, These last have wrought *but* one hour, and thou hast made them equal unto us, which have borne the burden and heat of the day.

13 But he answered one of them, and said, Friend, I do thee no wrong: didst not thou agree with me for a penny?

14 Take *that* thine *is,* and go thy way: I will give unto this last, even as unto thee.

15 Is it not lawful for me to do what I will with mine own? Is thine eye evil, because I am good?

16 So the last shall be first, and the first last: for many be called, but few chosen.

NOTES

God's Gracious Rewards

Lesson Text: Matthew 20:1-16

Related Scriptures: Matthew 19:16-30; 20:20-28; Luke 13:22-30

TIME: A.D. 30   PLACE: Perea

GOLDEN TEXT—"[The man] said unto them; Go ye also into the vineyard, and whatsoever is right I will give you. And they went their way" (Matthew 20:4).

Lesson Exposition

CALL TO THE LABORERS—Matt. 20:1-7

First shift of laborers (Matt. 20:1-2). The Gospel of Matthew contains numerous parables that Jesus used in His teaching ministry to clarify what He was teaching. Many of the parables began, "For the kingdom of heaven is like. . . ." These stories describe what is involved in living under God's rule.

The parable in this passage tells of a man who owned a large vineyard. At harvesttime he needed a number of laborers to pick the grapes. So he went out early in the morning to hire his workers. The standard wage for work like this was a "penny" (vs. 2), or a denarius, per day. The man and the laborers agreed to these terms, and he sent them into the vineyard at the beginning of the workday, which was about six o'clock in the morning.

Second shift of laborers (Matt. 20:3-4). After a few hours, the man realized that he needed more laborers. He went back to the marketplace around the third hour, or nine o'clock, and found some men there who were willing to work. Instead of agreeing on a set wage for them, the man promised to give them whatever was right.

Third and fourth shifts of laborers (Matt. 20:5). At noon and then again at three o'clock in the afternoon, the owner went back to the marketplace to get more workers. Each time, he found more available laborers to join those already in the vineyard. With these later shifts of laborers, he made the same vague agreement that he had made with the second shift.

Final shift of laborers (Matt. 20:6-7). The workday in ancient Israel ended around six o'clock in the evening. Just one hour before the end of the day, the owner recruited a final shift of workers. Once again, he did not set a specific wage for them.

COMPENSATION FOR THE LABORERS—Matt. 20:8-10

Procedure for wages (Matt. 20:8). When evening came, the owner gave his steward specific instructions about paying the laborers. This was a payday that was certain to be remembered by all the workers.

Payment to the final shift (Matt. 20:9). The first group to be paid were those who had begun last. No doubt they were prepared to receive about one-twelfth of a denarius, the proportional rate for their labor. When this last shift of workers came to the steward, they were amazed at the wage that they received. The owner had authorized them to get a full day's wage, a denarius. This was twelve times what they expected—or deserved.

The owner had compensated them according to his goodness, not according to what they had earned.

Payment to the first shift (Matt. 20:10). The first shift of workers knew what the group that had worked for only one hour had received. As they came before the steward, they reasoned that they would certainly receive more.

If the last shift had been surprised to get a full denarius, the first shift was stunned by receiving the same amount. The steward gave to them exactly what they had agreed to as a wage, no less and no more. Although in their own minds they supposed that they would receive more than the wages they had agreed to, that was not in fact the case.

COMPLAINT BY THE LABORERS — Matt. 20:11-16

Charge of unfairness (Matt. 20:11-12). The first-shift laborers began to grumble. The workers who had started later in the day had received much more per hour than they had. To their way of thinking, it seemed only right that they should be paid a bonus.

The earlier workers were offended that the latecomers were treated as well as they. Instead of rejoicing for the others, they insisted that those who had worked just one hour had no right to be compensated as the owner had determined. Consequently, those who had labored all day began to criticize the owner, accusing him of being unjust and unfair in his dealings.

Choice of grace (Matt. 20:13-14). Apparently the owner took one of the first-shift workers aside to talk with him. Because they had received the complete wage to which they had agreed, their charge of injustice could not be sustained. The owner had not defrauded them at all. He urged the worker to take his denarius and go his way rather than complain about it.

Challenge to gratitude (Matt. 20:15-16). The first workers spoke in terms of justice, but the owner gave in terms of grace. By their grumbling, the first workers were in effect saying that the owner was wrong for showing grace to others.

Jesus concluded the parable with the important lesson the story illustrated: "So the last shall be first, and the first last" (vs. 16). This reminded the disciples that while there is reward for faithful service to God, they must not think about it in strictly human terms. God gives freely according to His grace.

—*Daniel J. Estes.*

QUESTIONS

1. Why did Jesus use parables in describing the kingdom of heaven?
2. What agreement did the owner make with the first shift of workers?
3. How did the agreement with the later shifts differ from the first?
4. At what times of the day did the owner recruit workers?
5. How did the owner instruct the steward to pay the workers?
6. Why was the final shift of workers surprised at their wages?
7. Why were the first workers disappointed?
8. Why did the first workers murmur against the owner?
9. How did the owner show that their charge of injustice was not justified?
10. How does the parable illustrate God's grace to people?

—*Daniel J. Estes.*

PRACTICAL POINTS

1. It is the privilege of every Christian to be sent forth to labor for the Lord (Matt. 20:1-2).
2. We can be sure that our faithful service will be rewarded by the Lord (vss. 3-5).
3. Diligent, faithful service should characterize every Christian, regardless of his age or circumstances (vss. 6-7).
4. God's rewards are not based on the outward, superficial standards by which people often judge one another; He looks on the heart (vss. 8-13).
5. When we truly grasp the fact that all the blessings we enjoy are gifts of God's grace, there will be less place for envy (vss. 14-15).
6. It is senseless to follow the world's self-centered ways; they do not reflect the values of God (vs. 16).

—Jarl K. Waggoner.

RESEARCH AND DISCUSSION

1. What did all the vineyard workers in Jesus' parable have in common (Matt. 20:2-7)? How did they differ?
2. Does Jesus' parable suggest that our commonly held ideas about "fairness" are flawed (vss. 8-12)?
3. Are God's rewards for service exactly the same for all His children?
4. How should a Christian view his labor for the Lord and the Lord's rewards for such labor (vss. 13-15)?
5. In what ways can you illustrate the spiritual principle that "the last shall be first, and the first last" (vs. 16)?

—Jarl K. Waggoner.

Golden Text Illuminated

"[The man] said unto them; Go ye also into the vineyard, and whatsoever is right I will give you. And they went their way" (Matthew 20:4).

The Parable of the Laborers in the Vineyard has always provoked much comment. It has much to teach us about how God's ways are higher than our ways. Our golden text focuses on one of the ways this truth should affect out behavior.

After initially hiring some workers for his vineyard, the employer in the parable finds about three hours later that there are "others standing idle" (vs. 3), and so he hires them as well. The key part of the verse concerns the wages for these new workers. Instead of specifying how much they would receive, he simply says he will give them "whatsoever is right."

What this points to is one of the foundational teachings of Scripture—that we are to live our lives by faith in God. And this particular parable emphasizes that this faith includes trust in God's goodness.

By trusting in the fairness of the employer (who can again stand for God) these latecomers to the vineyard would enjoy the same benefits as those who were hired at the start.

At the heart of God's goodness is His grace. If we fail to understand that what we receive from God is not related to the extent or quality of our labor but instead to the simple free grace of the Saviour, we will find ourselves without a true grasp of who we are, who God is, and the only way we can have a relationship with Him.

—Stephen H. Barnhart.

LESSON 13   AUGUST 27, 2023

Scripture Lesson Text

LUKE 18:9 And he spake this parable unto certain which trusted in themselves that they were righteous, and despised others:

10 Two men went up into the temple to pray; the one a Pharisee, and the other a publican.

11 The Pharisee stood and prayed thus with himself, God, I thank thee, that I am not as other men *are,* extortioners, unjust, adulterers, or even as this publican.

12 I fast twice in the week, I give tithes of all that I possess.

13 And the publican, standing afar off, would not lift up so much as *his* eyes unto heaven, but smote upon his breast, saying, God be merciful to me a sinner.

14 I tell you, this man went down to his house justified *rather* than the other: for every one that exalteth himself shall be abased; and he that humbleth himself shall be exalted.

God's Great Mercy

Lesson Text: Luke 18:9-14

Related Scriptures: Matthew 18:1-5; 23:1-12;
Luke 16:14-17; Romans 3:10-30

TIME: A.D. 30   PLACE: on the way to Jerusalem

GOLDEN TEXT—"Every one that exalteth himself shall be abased; and he that humbleth himself shall be exalted" (Luke 18:14).

Lesson Exposition

ILLUSTRATION BY WAY OF PARABLE—Luke 18:9-10

A parable with a purpose (Luke 18:9). This chapter begins with two parables told by Jesus. In the first, He emphasized how important persistent prayer is; in the second, He contrasted the prayers of two people with entirely different attitudes. Jesus had a specific purpose in telling the first parable, and Luke spelled it out. "And He spake a parable unto them to this end, that men ought always to pray, and not to faint" (vs. 1).

The illustration Jesus used featured an emotionally impassive judge receiving a request from a woman who needed protection from an adversary. He finally acceded because of her persistence. Jesus followed this with another parable. Once again there was a purpose. There were those listening to Jesus who felt self-righteous to the degree that they were looking down on others they thought less spiritual.

This was especially an attitude of the religious leaders, who considered themselves to be the perfect examples of righteousness.

Two men with a purpose (Luke 18:10). Jesus began this parable by referring to two individuals who came to the temple to pray. The one was a prominent spiritual leader of the community and the other one of the most hated individuals in the community.

Jesus was again telling a parable with a specific purpose in mind. He began by stating that these two individuals had a purpose in attending the temple. Their purpose was to pray.

TWO ATTITUDES OF PRAYER—Luke 18:11-13

A prayer of pride (Luke 18:11-12). The Pharisees were meticulous about their religious practices, so it is no surprise that when this Pharisee arrived in the temple, he prayed. While he said he thanked God, there is really no element of praise in his prayer. Rather, what we read is an expression of self-exaltation! He used other people as his standard for righteousness rather than the standards of God and His demands.

His first words thanked God that he was not like other men. He immediately put all those who were not of his social and religious class in a category of inferiority and despicability.

He then pointed out specific areas in which he considered himself to be faithful in religious practice. He faithfully fasted twice a week (not just the required once), and he scrupulously tithed on everything. This was probably the truth. The problem in his doing of these things was that they were done with the wrong attitude.

A prayer of humility (Luke 18:13). The publican stood at a distance from the Pharisee, giving an indication that he felt most unworthy of being in the presence of God and the religious leader. He wanted to stay as separated as possible. Little did he realize that he was the more godly one and was keeping distant from one not approved by God! An additional evidence of his sincere humility is seen in the fact that he refused to even raise his eyes and look around him. He had genuine humility.

Furthermore, he stood and beat his chest, apparently as a physical indication of his recognition of the enormity of his sin and that it was keeping him at a distance from his God. It was an expression of his deep and sincere contrition. This man felt totally unworthy of being in God's presence. Unlike the Pharisee, his standard of comparison was God instead of other people. This gave him a more realistic evaluation.

The publican's prayer was that God might be merciful to him. He was asking God to see his repentant spirit and thus be satisfied with him. He had nothing else to offer.

APPLICATION OF THE PARABLE—Luke 18:14

It was the publican who went home justified in God's eyes, not the religious leader. Jesus simply referred to the Pharisee as the other person while He pointed out the one who was truly righteous at this point.

Being justified before God means being declared righteous and therefore innocent of all charges.

Humility is in the heart, where God looks to see what a person is really like, and which can be seen in its entirety only by God. God brings down those who are proud but exalts those who are genuinely humble. "Surely he scorneth the scorners: but he giveth grace unto the lowly" (Prov. 3:34).

Just as the Pharisee's outwardly pure life was no guarantee of salvation, neither is it so for any of the rest of us. It is only acknowledging our sinful condition and receiving Jesus as Saviour that will give us eternal life.

—Keith E. Eggert.

QUESTIONS

1. What did Jesus cover in the two parables He told?
2. Who were the two personalities Jesus used for His teaching in the second parable?
3. What was their purpose in going to the temple?
4. How did the Pharisee view himself, and what was his standard of comparison that led him to these conclusions?
5. How did the Pharisee emphasize how he viewed his religious activities?
6. What did the publican do to reveal a sense of unworthiness?
7. What was his prayer request?
8. What did Jesus declare about him and the Pharisee?
9. What does it mean that a person is justified?
10. What principle did Jesus state in Luke 18:14 about how God deals with people?

—Keith E. Eggert.

PRACTICAL POINTS

1. All self-righteousness is a matter of vastly misplaced trust (Luke 18:9).
2. If we look down on others with contempt, we can be sure our righteousness is not from God.
3. Praying to ourselves could be an apt description of what we do if we are not careful (vss. 10-11).
4. Too many public prayers are little more than thinly veiled bragging sessions (vs. 12).
5. We cannot approach a holy God without recognizing our need for mercy (vs. 13).
6. Humility is needed to avoid humiliation (vs. 14).

—Kenneth A. Sponsler.

RESEARCH AND DISCUSSION

1. Why is it so easy to think we are high up on the scale of righteousness and most other people are doing much worse (Luke 18:9)?
2. What was the reason for going to the temple to pray (vs. 10)? What modern equivalent might we follow today?
3. Few of us would likely be so obviously boastful in our prayers as the Pharisee was (vss. 11-12). In what subtle ways might we fall into such a trap?
4. If we know we have been saved by grace, do we still need to ask for God's mercy (vs. 13)? Why or why not?
5. How do we know we are being truly humble and not putting on a show of humility in order to be honored for it (vs. 14)?

—Kenneth A. Sponsler.

Golden Text Illuminated

"Every one that exalteth himself shall be abased; and he that humbleth himself shall be exalted" (Luke 18:14).

I was a good child. I went to church every week, was a good student, participated in many activities, and even volunteered on the side. I was also a braggart. I took pride in my accomplishments.

Like the Pharisee in the lesson, I was exalting myself. This Pharisee was someone with the highest standing in the temple. In contrast, the publican came from the lowest stratum of society. His occupation made him an outcast.

We find these two at the temple, praying. The Pharisee's prayer was an elaborate laundry list of his accomplishments. His prayer was all for show. The publican's prayer was sincere and honest. He merely asked that God show him mercy.

We know whose prayer God honored. Scripture tells us that it was the publican who went away forgiven that day. Why? The Pharisee's prayer was prideful and self-righteous. The publican's prayer was humble.

Proverbs 18:12 mentions that pride can bring about a person's downfall. We are also told that God resists the proud (Jas. 4:6).

Believers should lift others higher, not take a proud attitude and bring them down. As the old adage states, "There but for the grace of God go I."

Which person are you—self-righteous Pharisee or humble publican? Let us make practicing humility evidence of our authentic faith.

—Jennifer Lautermilch.

PARAGRAPHS ON PLACES AND PEOPLE

PEREA

Although not mentioned by this name in the Bible, this region east of the Jordan River has a rich biblical history. The area, called Gilead, was given to the tribes of Reuben, Gad, and Manasseh as an inheritance (Josh. 22:9). It is believed to be the same region where the prophet Elijah was from (I Kgs. 17:1). In the time of Christ's ministry, it was part of the territory ruled by Herod Antipas, and it is where John the Baptist preached and baptized (John 1:28-29). When Jews were traveling between Jerusalem and Galilee, the preferred route passed through this area to avoid Samaria. Many of Jesus' teachings and miracles took place here, "beyond Jordan" (Matt. 4:15, 25; Mark 3:8; John 3:26; 10:40).

ABRAHAM'S BOSOM

This place of comfort and blessing is spoken of by Jesus in the story of Lazarus and the rich man (Luke 16:22-23). Jewish apocryphal writings describe "Abraham's bosom" as a place of blessing in *Sheol* for those who are awaiting the final judgment. Those who were wicked, like the rich man, would be sent to Gehenna—a place of torment in *Sheol*—to await final judgment. The image Jesus painted may reflect the Jewish custom of reclining to eat with the most favored guest positioned next to the host, leaning on his bosom (cf. John 13:23). "Abraham's bosom" is also considered by many to be an alternative term for heaven, where the righteous ones of God await their resurrection.

THE MULTITUDES

In a general sense, the multitudes referred to in the Gospels were the crowds that followed Jesus (Matt. 4:25; Mark 5:24; Luke 12:1). Translated from the Greek word *ochlos,* "multitude" is found primarily in the Gospel accounts. When used, it was usually describing a gathering of the common people that did not have a specific leader (Matt. 9:36). The multitudes were amazed at Jesus' teaching and miracles (Matt. 9:8, 33; Mark 11:18; Luke 13:17). Jesus is recorded as having compassion for the multitudes (Matt. 15:32; Mark 8:2). This is in contrast to the religious leaders, who had disdain for the multitudes (cf. John 7:31, 32, 40-49). The multitudes were easily swayed to turn on Jesus at His trial, calling for His crucifixion (Matt. 27:20-25; Mark 15:11-13).

THE TWELVE

Jesus called twelve men to be His closest disciples (Mark 3:14-19). The number twelve matches the number of the twelve tribes of Israel and looks forward to the twelve foundations of the New Jerusalem (Rev. 21:14). These men were with Jesus day in and day out during His three-year ministry. They learned His ways and the ways of God's kingdom. Jesus ordained them and sent them out (Greek: *apostellō*) to preach, heal, and deliver the people of Israel in His name. Later this mission was expanded beyond Israel to include all people (Matt. 28:18-20). The names of all twelve men are given in three places: Matthew 10:2-4, Mark 3:16-19, and Luke 6:14-16. The Twelve are: Simon (Peter) and his brother Andrew, James and his brother John, Philip, Thomas, Bartholomew (Nathanael), Matthew (Levi), James (son of Alpheus), Thaddaeus (Judas the brother of James), Simon (the zealot), and Judas Iscariot. After Christ's ascension, Matthias was chosen to replace Judas Iscariot (Acts 1:13-26).

—*Kelly Hawver.*

Daily Bible Readings for Home Study and Worship

(Readings are for the week previous to the lesson topics.)

1. **June 4. Upside-Down Kingdom**
M —Comforted by Repentance. II Cor. 7:8-13.
T —Humility Draws God's Attention. Isa. 66:1-2.
W —New Heaven and New Earth. Rev. 21:1-4.
T —Suffering Prophets. Heb. 11:36-38.
F —Who Receives God's Blessing? Ps. 24:1-6.
S —The Beatitudes. Luke 6:20-26.
S —Who Are Kingdom Citizens? Matt. 5:1-16.

2. **June 11. A Perfect Kingdom**
M —Unbelieving Israel. Rom. 9:30—10:4.
T —Building on the Foundation of Christ. I Cor. 3:11-15.
W —Mercy over Judgment. Jas. 2:10-13.
T —Common Grace. Acts 14:8-18.
F —God Hates Evil. Ps. 5:4-8.
S —Understanding God's Laws. Matt. 5:31-37.
S —God's Standard for His Kingdom. Matt. 5:17-18, 21-22, 27-28, 38-39, 43-44.

3. **June 18. A Victorious Kingdom**
M —A House Divided. Matt. 12:22-32.
T —Jesus Overpowers Satan. Luke 11:14-23.
W —Sin That Leads to Death. I John 5:14-17.
T —The Twelve Are Sent. Matt. 10:1-15.
F —The Seventy-Two Sent. Luke 10:1-12.
S —Lord of the Sabbath. Luke 6:1-5.
S —Authority over Satan. Mark 3:13-19; 6:6b-13.

4. **June 25. Growing God's Kingdom**
M —Small Beginnings. Mark 4:26-32.
T —Increasing Influence. Luke 13:18-21.
W —Setting Up God's Kingdom. Dan. 2:24-47.
T —The Returning Christ. Matt. 24:29-31.
F —Evil Removed from the World. Matt. 13:36-43.
S —The Final Harvest. Rev. 14:14-20.
S —Good and Evil Grow Together. Matt. 13:24-33.

5. **July 2. Praying to God**
M —Song of Praise. I Chr. 16:23-34.
T —Extolling the Lord. Ps. 145:1-21.
W —Daily Bread for Israel. Ex. 16:15-22.
T —Seeking the Face of the Lord. Ps. 27:7-14.
F —All Are Unrighteous. Rom. 3:10-20.
S —Honest Prayer. Matt. 6:5-8.
S —Teach Us to Pray. Luke 11:1-13.

6. **July 9. Accept God's Invitation!**
M —Unprepared for the Kingdom. Matt. 22:1-14.
T —The Stone Rejected. Matt. 21:42-44.
W —Gospel Scorned by the Jews. Acts 13:44-52.
T —A Place of Honor. Prov. 25:6-7.
F —The Proud Will Be Humbled. Isa. 2:10-12.
S —Hospitality to the Poor. Luke 14:12-14.
S —Two Critical Warnings. Luke 14:7-11, 15-24.

7. **July 16. A Warning for the Hard-Hearted**
M —What Does Your Heart Treasure? Matt. 6:19-21.
T —Give to the Poor. Luke 12:32-34.
W —Heavenly Treasure. Mark 10:17-22.
T —Judgment of the Dead. Rev. 20:11-15.
F —The Lake of Fire. Rev. 21:5-8.
S —Unbelieving Hearts. Heb. 3:7-19.
S —The Rich Man and Lazarus. Luke 16:19-31.

8. **July 23. Separating the Sheep and the Goats**
M —Authority Given to the Son of Man. Dan. 7:9-14.
T —A Coming Judgment. Matt. 16:24-28.
W —Judging the World in Righteousness. Ps. 9:1-10.
T —Evidence of Faith. Jas. 2:14-20.
F —Pure Religion. Jas. 1:22-27.
S —God Judges Rightly. II Thess. 1:3-10.
S —Judgment of the Nations. Matt. 25:31-46.

9. **July 30. Ears to Hear**
M —Listen to My Instruction. Ps. 78:1-8.
T —Receiving God's Word. Matt. 13:18-23.
W —Hearing Without Understanding. Isa. 6:8-12.
T —Revealed Mystery of Christ. Rom. 16:25-27.
F —Taught by the Spirit. I Cor. 2:6-16.
S —Imperishable Seed. I Pet. 1:22-25.
S —Hearing God's Word. Matt. 13:9-17.

10. **August 6. Forgiving One Another**
M —Love and Forgive Enemies. Luke 6:27-38.
T —Much Love with Much Forgiveness. Luke 7:36-50.
W —Mercy to the Unfaithful. Ps. 78:32-40.
T —Called to Forgive. Col. 3:12-17.
F —Always Willing to Forgive. Luke 17:3-4.
S —Forgiveness Through the Blood. Eph. 1:3-10.
S —Repeated Forgiveness. Matt. 18:21-35.

11. **August 13. A Story of Forgiveness**
M —Firstborn's Portion. Deut. 21:15-17.
T —Grace of the Father. Matt. 7:7-12.
W —Prayer for Mercy. Ps. 86:1-7.
T —Turn from Sin and Live. Ezek. 18:21-23.
F —Welcome the Repentant. Luke 15:25-32.
S —God Will Comfort the Repentant. Isa. 57:15-21.
S —Repentance and Reconciliation. Luke 15:11-24.

12. **August 20. God's Gracious Rewards**
M —A Rich Man's Sorrow. Matt. 19:16-22.
T —Salvation Only by God's Grace. Matt. 19:23-30.
W —Beware of Envy. Jas. 3:13-18.
T —The Last Will Be First. Luke 13:22-30.
F —God Will Assign Us Our Place. Matt. 20:20-23.
S —Not Demanding Our Privileges. Matt. 17:24-27.
S —God's Grace Illustrated. Matt. 20:1-16.

13. **August 27. God's Great Mercy**
M —No Place for Boasting. Rom. 3:21-26.
T —Fast in Secret. Matt. 6:16-18.
W —God Knows the Heart. Luke 16:13-15.
T —The Proud Humbled. Matt. 23:1-12.
F —Faith like a Child's. Matt. 18:1-5.
S —Turn from False Worship. Isa. 1:10-17.
S —Humble Faith. Luke 18:9-14.